Playing Bigger Than You Are

A Life in Organizing

Playing Bigger Than You Are

A Life in Organizing

by Stewart Acuff

For Kathleen,

Thanks for your commitment!

Levins Publishing

Cover art by CD Design, Ltd.

Text design and production by Elizabeth Edwards and BookMobile Design and Publishing Services.

Permission granted by Susan Wells to use the poem on the final page.
It first appeared in the book *Changing Course: Windcall and the Art of Renewal* by Susan Wells, Heyday Press, 2007.

Levins Publishing
2300 Kennedy Street NE
Suite 160
Minneapolis, Minnesota 55413
612-238-0989
www.LevinsPublishing.com

Distributed by Itasca Books
www.itascabooks.com

ISBN 978-0-9853972-2-7
LCCN 2012938182

*For my brothers and sisters
at the Utility Workers Union of America,
for my friend and colleague D. Michael Langford,
and for my family:
Dad, Sam, Sydney, and Mary Kaye*

Acknowledgments

I AM grateful to my editor, Jane Dickerson, for greatly improving my prose without taking it out of my voice. I am sincerely grateful to my publisher for seeking me out and giving me this wonderful opportunity to write. I am very proud to work for the Utility Workers Union of America, a grassroots oriented, militant union that fights everyday for all workers. I am proud to be an organizer, part of our labor movement, and to be able to live my values and convictions. As always, I am grateful to all those organizers and leaders and campaigners I've learned from all these many years and those I continue to learn from. Many are named in this book, but there are far too many to catalog them all. I am very grateful for the wonderful love of my family. I am grateful for both this journey and all I've learned along the way. And I am especially grateful to you for picking up this book. I sincerely hope you enjoy it.

Foreword

I first met Stewart Acuff when he came to Vermont for an International Human Rights Day rally in December of 2003. A snowy weekend slowed us down enough to have more time together than such events usually allow. He listened more than he spoke, but his passion for workers and their rights was clear. He was prepared to undertake a massive national campaign for passage of the Employee Free Choice Act and wanted me on board. I was, and still am.

Over time, Stewart and I became friends. We have shared some proud moments together. I recall the time in my Senate office when Stewart watched me sign an agreement between McDonald's and a farm workers' organization in South Florida called the Coalition for Immokalee Workers. The workers gained improved pay and working conditions. Though the document was signed in Washington, it was clear that the struggle had been waged—and won—by organizing in the fields in Florida. At that time, I gained a greater appreciation for Stewart as an organizer for justice. It is all too easy to think of Washington as a center of power. Stewart knows that power flows everywhere there are organized Americans, and he is one of the best when it comes to helping Americans organize to get things done.

Today, America is locked in a bitter struggle between organized people and organized money. The very simple political reality is that those of us in Congress who are prepared to stand up to organized money will not be successful without the strong support of millions of Americans at the grassroots level. Equally true is the reality that the average American citizen—disgusted with tax breaks for billionaires, Wall Street greed, a never-ending recession, attacks on Social Security, two wars and minimal efforts against global warming—will not see his or her views translated into legislation without the support of organized people. Without the support of organized people, we progressives in Congress are no match for organized money.

Never in my lifetime has more been at stake. In the midst of the worst recession since the Great Depression of the 1930s, the middle class is collapsing and poverty is increasing. Meanwhile, the people at the top are doing phenomenally well. The crooks on Wall Street whose greed precipitated this recession are now earning more money than before the American people bailed them out. The top one percent in our country now earn over 23 percent of all income, more than the bottom 50 percent. The U.S. today has by far the most unequal distribution of income and wealth of any major country on earth and the gap between the very rich and everyone else is growing wider.

While "official" unemployment is at 9.8 percent, real unemployment is over 16 percent—and even higher for blue collar workers. Despite massive unemployment and the collapse of the middle class, the representatives of organized money want more tax breaks for the wealthy, more government deregulation, more unfettered free trade, more anti-union legislation and—as if this was not bad enough—they want an end of funding for unemployment benefits.

Playing Bigger Than You Are is not a discussion and analysis of the issues we face. Stewart did that in his last book, *Getting America Back To Work*. Nor is it a manual on how to organize, which I hear Stewart may have simmering on his mind's back burner. No, it is more than either of these. It is the day-to-day story of a life in organizing, a life dedicated to justice for all Americans. Be it organizing citizens for stop signs at a busy intersection in Memphis, struggling to unionize the Atlanta Olympics, or guiding the nationwide organizing program of the AFL-CIO, we see in these pages a man with an uncanny mix of theory, compassion, and courage. We see a man trying to hide his disappointment when campaigns go badly, and heaping credit on others when success comes calling. We see a man living what his country preacher father taught him, that we are all, every one of us, deserving of respect and dignity.

Playing Bigger Than You Are is above all a story of hope's triumph against all odds. At this challenging time in our nation's history it is a story we can learn much from.

Senator Bernie Sanders
Burlington, Vermont
September 2011

Introduction

IN MY previous book, *Getting America Back To Work*, I talked about a 30-year assault by the Financial Elite on America's working families. This was no accident, nor was it inevitable. Instead, it was a deliberate, organized program to slash wages and benefits, to lower our standard of living, and to shift wealth toward the few at the top and away from everyone else. As I write this, the fruits of that effort, measured in millions of middle class dreams turned to nightmares, are now upon us. This is what organized money can do and has done.

I also wrote about the antidote to the power of organized money, which is the power of organized people. Over and over, history tells us that organized people can change the world. My own life is filled with too many examples for me to believe otherwise. I have seen organized people do something as simple as get a foot-dragging city council to put up a stop sign in a poor neighborhood or something as grand as derailing a Presidential candidacy. I have seen organized people demand, and get, better access to health care. I have seen them come away from bargaining tables with better wages and benefits than anyone had thought possible. And I have seen the beginnings of an international movement that, when it comes to full power, will restore sanity to world trade policies.

In truth, I owe the fact that I am here to write this book at all to the power of organized people. I was raised in West Tennessee and Southeast Missouri. On one side of my family, my grandfather was a farmer who earned the money to buy his farm by skidding cypress, oak, and hickory trees out of the Mississippi River swamps and bottomlands with his team of oxen. Until he died when I was six, my parents took me to his fields to pick cotton and gather it into the tiny sack they had made me from an empty flour sack. On the other side of my family, my grandmother was the daughter of a sharecropper and tenant farmer. She and her family never owned a thing. They lived in dirt poverty and were totally dependent on the plantation owners.

My future changed once and for all when my grandmother, her husband, and my cousins moved to St. Louis. There they found the power of organized people in the union jobs that allowed them to crawl out of poverty and into the middle class that sustained and educated me. That middle class didn't just happen. Organized people built it. And because they built it, a child of Scots-Irish, Native American, and African American ancestry, who was destined to repeat the cycle of brutal Southern poverty, rose to a wonderful life as an organizer for social change.

You can't be raised in the midst of that much poverty by the parents I was blessed with, one a teacher and the other a Southern Baptist preacher, without developing concern and compassion for average people. My faithful reading of the Bible and daily prayers convinced me that God loves all people, that all people as children of God are worthy of dignity and respect, and that racism violated God's will. The conflict between Southern mores and the scriptures turned many young Southerners, me included, into activists. How to channel that activism into change? For me, the answers came from Professor John Galliher during my college days at the University of Missouri, from my lifelong friend Bob Arnold, and from reading Si Kahn's first book, *How People Get Power*. The best way to fight poverty and human misery was to organize average people so they could build their collective power to get a fair share of the wealth they produced. Thus began my life's work, a struggle filled with deep joy, one devoted to helping people build power.

Now I find myself in a different position. More times than I can count, a person much younger than I am will approach me at a rally or after a speech I have given. They'll ask the simple question, "How do you do it?" They know the answer lies in organization, and have chosen to devote their lives to the task of building power for social change. But that question, "How do you do it?" looms large. I want so much for these young people to succeed, for the future of our nation lies in their hands. So, in this book, I will try to answer their question as best I can. I will tell you my story, and how I did it.

For over thirty years, I learned organizing by doing it on the streets and dirt roads of America and in some far more lavish settings, too. I have organized for community groups, for political groups, and for labor groups. I have seen great victories that sustained me and endured crushing defeats that even today leave their scars. For part of this book, I will tell you that story. It won't be your story, or the way you will do it, but it will show you how one person did it. It will show you how much work it is to knock on doors day in and day out, how grueling the travel can be, and how sweet the victories taste. Then, I will tell you some of the lessons I have taken with me from those years on the streets. To be successful, there are things you must know. There are things you must do. And, most importantly, there are things you must believe.

It has been a long time, what seems like a lifetime ago, since I was a young ACORN organizer reading

Saul Alinsky's *Rules for Radicals*. I can only hope that your reading this book will have the same effect reading Alinsky's book had on me. Even more, I can only hope that your life will in some ways be as fulfilling as mine has been.

She lowered her head when she spoke
Looking at hands and fingers thick from work
As if she were reading or studying those hands
Which raised her children and the children of others
Took care of the sick and helpless
Those hands provided everything
She spoke low and soft as when ashamed
you couldn't protect your own dignity
Listening with every part of me
Reminding her that dignity can be recovered
With a fight

1

Starting Out

I PULLED UP to the Dallas ACORN office just before midnight in July of 1977. Prostitutes worked the shadows of Ross Avenue while used car dealers, one after the other, cried out to all who passed by, "Goss on Ross! He's the Trading Hoss!" I had just graduated from the University of Missouri and recently finished my first organizing training campaign in working class suburban St. Louis. But all of that seemed a long way away as I stepped out of the 15-year-old Pontiac my father had given me.

I was introduced to community organizing while at Missouri by my friend, Bob Arnold, and by Si Kahn's book, *How People Get Power*. As my senior year wore down I decided to try out community organizing. I had developed a Christianity-based commitment to social, economic, and racial justice. The Association for Community Organizations for Reform Now (ACORN, for short) was organizing in tough places very close to the ground. I did my training organizing drive in an old inner ring working class suburb of St. Louis. Shortly after the training drive, I was on my way to Dallas.

Stephen Holt, who was to become a lifelong friend and mentor, was waiting for me. In short order, I found myself working in Oak Cliff, a diverse, working class area separated from the rest of Dallas by the Trinity River. Now began my real education. I learned to knock on 40 doors daily between four in the afternoon and eight at night. I learned how to move folks to action to get stop signs in their neighborhoods or get a burned-out house torn down to stop neighborhood blight. I learned how to get the average Texan to march on the Public Utilities Commission for lower electric rates. And, throughout it all, I slowly learned the toughest lesson of all: organizing is not about doing things for people. No. Organizing is about teaching people how to do things for themselves. It's about building power.

A co-worker taught me that if you wanted to find the best neighborhood leaders, you needed to look for the houses with the most flowers in the yard. A woman named Bessie Meeks, chair of the Beckley-Sanor Neighborhood Association, had a very nice yard. She and her husband, both white and in their 70's, lived in a mostly African-American and Latino community. I never heard or sensed the least bit of racism or discrimination in either of them.

Bessie was always there. She chaired every community meeting, spoke at every city meeting, and was a great cook, to boot. Every time I went to her house, a wonderful meal was waiting for me. I remember country fried steak with lots of gravy, delicious vegetables cooked in fat, Southern-style, like my mother made them, greens, beans, and jalapeno cornbread. The Bible says that it is not by bread alone that we live. Maybe so, but when you are out on the streets, living poor, a good meal goes a long way toward keeping your spirit alive.

I was blessed with great teachers during the six months I worked in Dallas. Stephen Holt, Scott Holladay, Louise Archuleta, and, of course, Bessie Meeks, come to mind. Stephen was head organizer of Texas ACORN and my boss. Scott, my co-worker, was also a street organizer, my roommate, and very soon a close friend. Mrs. Archuleta, an angry, aging woman of Mexican-American and Apache descent, wagged and waved her finger at city council members, state public utilities commissioners, and anyone and everyone we opposed. She was unforgettable and powerful. Together, we won streetlights and sidewalk repairs, and then attacked redlining banks for their refusal to make home loans in low and moderate-income minority neighborhoods.

ACORN was not a perfect organization. None are. But it was perfect for me—the perfect place to shake off the dust of academia and begin my life on the streets. Its members were the very salt of the earth. Its leaders were the kind of people who were pastors and deacons in small, neighborhood churches. Neighbors looked to them when they needed help. The staff, all battle-hardened warriors for justice, believed we could change America if only we knocked on enough doors and engaged enough people. And, of course, they were right.

The ACORN folks must have seen something in me, because after six months, at the tender age of twenty-three, I was back in the old Pontiac. This time, I was rolling toward Memphis to take over as head organizer for Tennessee ACORN. Life in Memphis started on the night of my birthday, December 17, at a bar called the Buccaneer. Jon Beam, my predecessor, and his wife met me and filled me in on the new government Volunteers in Service to America (VISTA) grant that had helped ACORN grow at the national level from 35 to about 200 staff persons. Twenty of those new people were organizers assigned to me in Memphis. The grant meant a little more money in my pocket, too. Instead of the fifty dollars a week we all made before the grant, we were knocking down a princely sixty-three a week. It was the lowest weekly wage that VISTA allowed.

Direct action and grassroots demonstrations were ACORN's most important tactics to draw attention to and find solutions to injustices and inequities in poor and working class communities. These actions were often creative and/or boisterous. They included everything from sitting in at a city official's office to mass turnout and testimony at a city council meeting or hearing to filling a bank lobby with low-income people to protest redlining. These actions were a way to give collective voice and direction to the anger of poor and working class people in a way to force those with power to right wrongs and balance inequities.

Much to his credit, Jon Beam had built a culture of militancy in Memphis that served us well. We took over city offices to get a more equitable distribution of Housing for Urban Development funds for neighborhood improvement. We sat in at the office of Memphis Light, Gas, and Water as we fought to lower utility rates for poor people. We fought against lending discrimination by banks and for better and safer neighborhoods and communities in Memphis. These actions, and many like them, showed me the importance of accepting conflict. It's important to understand that those who are most comfortable with conflict and confrontation will win the most battles and will be confronted the least.

Through all this, I struggled mightily to learn how to supervise 20 organizers and oversee a citywide community organization. In addition, my apartment had no air conditioning, so on many a summer night I sat on the banks of the Mississippi River enjoying the breezes that came off the water, fighting ferocious mosquitoes, nursing a quart of beer or malt liquor, and generally trying to cool off and relax from the day's trials. There were always tests and challenges, but one especially stands out.

I arrived back at the ACORN office to finish my day on a hot, Mississippi river hot, Sunday afternoon after a staff retreat in a state park. Four middle-aged men in suits were waiting outside in what had to be a burning hot parked car. Of course, I wondered who they were as I drove up. They promptly produced badges and announced that two were congressional investigators and two were officials from VISTA investigating the ACORN grant. My co-worker, a young African-American woman from Philadelphia named Terese Bouey, had refused to let them into our office.

Terese was tough, so I wasn't surprised that she'd left our unwanted guests to bake in their car while waiting for me to show up. First I conferred with Terese, then invited them inside. They flashed badges again and said they were there to investigate misuse of federal funds. After getting their permission, I called one of the ACORN lawyers who advised me to tell the truth. I asked if I could quote the Bible, and he said, "Of course." I had prayed and read the Bible every night through high school and college. As I read it, it became clear to me that Jesus of Nazareth, the itinerant, penniless carpenter, prophet, and Savior was no tool of the Romans, the elders, or the financial elite.

Thus, as these investigators began their interrogation, I responded whenever I could with scripture. I treated them to a discourse on the meaning of Matthew 25: "Inasmuch as you have done it unto the least of these, you have also done it to me." I told them of Paul's letter to the Romans: "Overcome evil with good." I expounded on the prophesy of Jeremiah and Isaiah in the Old Testament. As you might imagine, it wasn't long before they concluded that the best view of Memphis was through their car's rearview mirror. I learned that Sunday that courage is action to overcome fear, not a feeling to replace fear. I learned that we get to choose fear or courage. We can be overcome with fear, or we can overcome fear with action and courage.

While working for ACORN I experienced what it is to live in abject poverty. I ate bologna and peanut butter, greens and beans. I developed a great dish of scrambled eggs for protein, diced potatoes to fill the belly, and onions and hot sauce for flavor. Having the ACORN organizers live on fifty to sixty-five dollars a week stretched out the resources of the organization, allowing us to put more organizers on the street, organize more communities and cities, and build a more powerful organization. But that staff poverty also forced all of us young organizers to taste and experience life as many of the people we were organizing did.

In Memphis in 1978 neither my office nor my apartment nor my car had air conditioning. Several of my staff and I sold blood once a week for ten dollars a pint. From there we went to an all-you-can-eat pizza buffet where we gorged ourselves. No one had a T V, so we frequented dollar movies and the cheapest bars in town. In the bars, we drank as slowly as we could from a quart of malt liquor, sipping to make it last as long as possible. We seldom went out to eat, and then usually to family places in the communities where we worked, like Mexican and barbecue places in Dallas or barbecue or soul food in Memphis. But mostly, we all became very creative cooks. We learned why the best food in the world was peasant food. And we ate with our members as often as we could. I sometimes went to see the Memphis Chicks minor league baseball team during the seventh inning because you could get in free for the last two or three innings. And we worked long hours, leaving the office at 9 to 10 p.m., giving us very little time to think about what our poverty denied us.

One day I was playing basketball at the YMCA with a group of intense players, almost all of them with college experience. I caught a hard elbow on the side of my nose and the bone broke through the skin under my eye. We drove to the county hospital emergency room. Poor as we were, we didn't think of going anywhere else. I'd played high school and street or playground basketball since I was 12 years old. I'd had stitches in my eyebrows, split lips, cuts on my forehead and chin, but nothing like a bone sticking out of my face. I found myself waiting in line behind 73 people in a hospital emergency room, hurting like hell. Life in poverty is hard.

In Memphis I learned about courage and conflict and confrontation. Between Dallas and Memphis, I'd learned that average Americans would work together to build power and could accomplish amazing things. I'd also learned about fear and pain and discomfort. I'd learned that the house call, the home visit, the door knock were the central skills in organizing. I'd learned that listening and validating people's anger and pain was more important than long discourses on social policy. Mostly, though, I learned the extraordinary power of collective action, the power of folks working together.

In the fall of 1978, I decided to leave organizing to pursue an academic career and be with my college sweetheart. I moved back to St. Louis and got a job moving furniture. After saving some money, I transferred to Chicago where Catherine was in graduate school at the University of Chicago. We both had changed since those sweet days at Missouri University, and the relationship soon ended.

Back I went back to St. Louis where my former employer put me in an 18-wheeler moving van hauling households all over America and even Canada. It was incredibly hard work, moving furniture all day long and driving half the night, but it allowed me to put a little cash together.

I drove that truck until August of 1979 when I showed up at the University of Michigan to begin a doctorate program in political science, lasting all of five days before I hit the road again.

2

New Hampshire

OF ALL the places a son of the rural South least expected to live, New Hampshire would have topped the list. My Pontiac had long since died and I was hitchhiking where I could, riding buses where I couldn't, to visit friends and family. I'd been to see my brother Stephen, my best old friend Bob Arnold, and Cousin Janice, Aunt Lorraine, and Uncle Milburn in New Jersey. I planned to travel this way till the money ran out, working when I had to, while I figured out what to do with my life. My travels eventually took me to Woodville, New Hampshire, late in the summer of 1979 to visit friend and mentor Stephen Holt from Texas and his family. I planned to hang out with him and his family for a couple of weeks, then split before it got cold in New Hampshire. Instead, I stayed for three years.

Holt moved on from ACORN to head a new state-wide community organization called the New Hampshire

People's Alliance. We talked about organizing and sports, mainly the Red Sox, Celtics, and Patriots, while I fell in love with New Hampshire and Vermont. One night when Stephen and his wife went out for a while, I stayed in to watch their kids, Adrienne and Moriah. I began reading *A Passion for Equality*, a new biography of George Wiley, the founder of the Welfare Rights Organization. I read all night. I couldn't put it down. The next morning I told Holt I would stay and organize for the New Hampshire People's Alliance.

Holt was nothing if not visionary and organizationally ambitious. I worked with staff members Jim Hexter, Nancy Cole, and Ellen Fleischmann to hold town hall meetings, small coffees, and gatherings all over the state to sound out New Hampshire's low and moderate-income people on national issues. As a result, we created a statewide New Hampshire People's Agenda in the run-up to the primaries before the presidential election in 1980. We probed what issues had the power to improve the lives of poor and working class people:

- the cost of energy and heat,
- tax policy favoring average people instead of the corporations,
- effective services for poor people,
- more effective federal food programs.

And as we discussed these policies, average people in New Hampshire allowed themselves to think about what an American government focused on the needs of its most vulnerable, instead of its most powerful, could do for its own people

I learned a lot about consensus building in the process. I also learned how to listen. I listened hard for points of agreement during discussions, asking Socratic questions to get agreement on a point or a policy. I listened actively, watching every face in a room to see which ideas were hitting home. I listened with my eyes and ears and developed a kind of antenna for social dynamics that would serve me well for the rest of my career.

I also learned the value of what Holt called "playing bigger than you are." It means how to fill the void where ordinary Americans aren't heard. That notion worked when we took on the state public utilities commission. We won lower residential utility rates, a winter utility shut-off rule, and a policy to keep hydroelectric power generated in New Hampshire. Our organization made the lives of hundreds and thousands of people in New Hampshire safer and better during long, frigid winters. Eventually, the U.S. Supreme Court struck down our policy on hydroelectric power, but not before we packed that court's chambers with low and moderate-income people bearing silent witness to the justice of our policy.

I spent most of my time in New Hampshire organizing in Claremont, an old industrial mill town on the Connecticut River. Even though it was a rural town of only about 13,000, Claremont had a certain urban feel because of all the factories and industries from the paper mill to the steel mill and everything in between. Soon I was treated as a colleague by the union organizers and representatives in town. Several became leaders in our local chapter of the New Hampshire People's Alliance.

Claremont was the place I became a lifelong organizer. We built a strong local community organization that fought for better city services, against increases in water rates, and for the development of local hydroelectric power. Statewide, we ran a campaign to force corporations operating in New Hampshire to pay their fair share in state taxes. We called the campaign "Share the Wealth." Holt wrote a brilliant ten-page memo outlining the campaign, its rationale, and the inequity of New Hampshire's tax policy.

Someone, no doubt upset with our organization, gave Holt's memo to the state's notoriously conservative statewide newspaper. One morning we woke to find the entire memo, starting with half the front page and continuing to an entire jump page, in the *Manchester Union-Leader*. The memo was accompanied by a front-page editorial headlined, "Try a Little Tenderness." It was a cruel and ironic twist on Otis Redding's great soul song. To put it mildly, it was a helluva shock. We had become a power in the state, strong enough to not only challenge the status quo, but to change it as well. More ominously, powerful interests were showing us they would do extraordinary things to stop the New Hampshire People's Alliance. It was both gratifying and extremely sobering.

We continued the campaign, but the *Union-Leader* had hijacked an effort meant to establish some sense of equity and tax justice and had given it nefarious motives and subversive potential. The mood of the country and New Hampshire was changing; then came the election of Ronald Reagan and the implementation of his conservative agenda. Funding for our work was cut back drastically. I often thought about organizing somewhere else, but quitting never crossed my mind. By then, I was an organizer through and through.

In five years of community organizing in St. Louis, Dallas, Memphis, and New Hampshire, I had acquired all the primary skills of an effective organizer. I had become competent and comfortable in the work and had acquired the personal toughness the work demanded. I had learned to accept inherent conflict and rejection by savoring the sweetness of victories. I was an organizer, though I must admit I didn't know then it would be a lifelong vocation and passion.

3

Back to Texas

NOT LONG after Ronald Reagan's election as President in 1980, much of the financial assistance for community organizing groups like the New Hampshire People's Alliance began to dry up. Private foundations felt compelled to fund direct services instead. Most of our contributions in New Hampshire to the People's Alliance disappeared. Another veteran community organizer, Bill Pastreich, who'd moved on to union organizing, told me about an exciting campaign and opportunity to organize some of the most exploited workers in America into unions. The Service Employees International Union (SEIU) was beginning a campaign to organize the workers at Beverly Enterprises Nursing Homes.

In October of 1982 the Service Employees Union was not nearly as well known as it is today. John Sweeney had only recently come on as president of the union. I was the first organizer he hired. SEIU wanted to organize more and build a movement union. A strategic organizing campaign at America's largest nursing home chain, Beverly Enterprises, was just beginning. Except for quick stops in Rhode Island and St. Louis, SEIU sent me almost immediately to Houston. Once there, I was put in charge of the campaign to organize Beverly nursing homes in Texas.

When I arrived in East Texas and Houston in late 1982, Ronald Reagan was halfway through his first term and the United States was in one of its conservative moments. Funding cuts had not yet crippled community organizing. The American labor movement had not yet opened to those from the outside who shared the values of worker power and workplace justice. East Texas, to boot, was still a bastion of the Ku Klux Klan; Vidor, just outside Beaumont, was home to one of the Grand Wizards.

By contrast, Houston was a wonderful polyglot of working class culture—Tejano, Creole including wonderful Zydeco music at the Creole Catholic school fundraisers, white country and Texas ethnic, southern Black. But rural East Texas felt a lot like the rural south of my boyhood. The barbecue was beef instead of pork, but it was very good. Black people were oppressed in every imaginable way. The worst jobs were reserved for Black women. They made the minimum wage or just over it at the nursing homes we wanted to organize.

When I started organizing in Palestine, about 150 miles north of Houston, Mae Nell and Etra Mae had to teach me how to drive and navigate the pure sand road to their house. Directions to workers' homes commonly included, "When you see the blackjack oak look for your next left." It was the South that I knew and that of which William Faulkner had said, "The past is never dead. It's not even past."

After putting together a coalition of support and a small crew of organizers, we began workers' outreach in 1983. By the end of 1984, our crew had organized nursing homes in places like Nacogdoches, Beaumont, Liberty, Palestine, Texas City, and Bryan. The nursing home staff was almost all African-American workers. We organized them all through the complicated National Labor Relations Board process in spite of heavy, even withering, employer retaliations and intimidation. These wonderful women in Texas were not only building power for themselves. Because of their determination, they added their power to that of workers in high union density cities like Philly, Detroit, and San Francisco. Every newly organized workplace became part of the struggle to negotiate a national, master contract.

At the Beverly nursing homes newly represented by the SEIU, bosses had to respect their employees or face a grievance and questioning from Beverly's corporate leaders. These women had changed the game and the way the bosses talked to and treated them. The power they won on the job gave them the confidence and courage and sisterly solidarity to confront more personal problems. Their biggest rewards came from their newfound sense of personal and collective empowerment and they began to assert their dignity in their personal lives. They learned to stand up to their men or husbands. Some left abusive relationships. They were no longer the doormats too many of them had been their whole lives. They gained a whole new sense of self-respect. This, more than anything, is what sustained me during those tough Texas days and nights.

Workers in unorganized nursing homes, however, continued to be threatened day after day. Captive audience meetings were brutal. The African-American and Creole women workers were harassed daily in one-on-one sessions and captive audience meetings where they were repeatedly threatened with losing their jobs and livelihoods. Typically, union busting law firms and consultants and their management clients attempt to intimidate, retaliate, and scare workers from their union. Management often created captive audience meetings where whole shifts were pulled into a mass meeting meant to terrify workers away from the union. Workers were also pulled into one-on-one supervisory sweat sessions. At the Beverly Home in Nacogdoches, our key leader was required to sit in the cafeteria right in the middle of the facility where everyone could see and hear. The nursing home superintendent and the Beverly regional director then proceeded to scream at her for two hours.

My life was threatened three times in six months. In Nacogdoches, the local NAACP chairman warned us about the Ku Klux Klan. The warning was not without merit. One night they called me at my motel and threatened to "cut me from asshole to appetite." I'm still not exactly clear what that meant, but I was quite sure I didn't want to find out through personal experience! Still we carried on. Between our small staff and our allies like the Chicano group of Brown Berets, we leafleted dozens of nursing homes in east and central Texas with a survey about working conditions, pay, and benefits. We got scores of calls.

We also relied on strong, well-educated committees and intense weekly house calls. That meant visiting every worker every week. We out-communicated the bosses and set the SEIU record for twelve straight NLRB victories without a defeat. We began to build leadership and organizing communities where we could find and identify worker leaders.

4

On to Atlanta

A NEW opportunity arose in 1985. President Sweeney
and Andy Stern asked me to move to Atlanta to start
the Georgia State Employees Union Local 1985 of SEIU.
I was more than happy to accept the assignment. I had
dreamed of both heading and building a local union.
Now, both would happen together. And what native
Southerner doesn't want to someday find himself or her-
self in Atlanta, the commercial and cultural capital of the
South? It wasn't long before I learned how big a challenge
this assignment would be. Unions weren't recognized,
there was no provision for dues check off, and the state's
attorney general wrote the opinion that public employee
collective bargaining violated the state constitution. We
thus were reduced to the fundamental definition, obliga-
tion, and function of a labor union: a vehicle for workers'
collective power.

In the absence of collective bargaining and any other form of structured communication between the workers and those who controlled their work lives, we created space and opportunity for that communication to take place. We took over state department commissioners' offices, always taking with us state legislators like Tyrone Brooks and Nan Orrock, to force a discussion on working conditions and issues. These actions were, of course, illegal—criminal trespassing—but we were very careful to not have only rank-and-file members arrested. Leadership participated, too. Our actions were one way to approximate collective bargaining.

We were the first union of corrections officers in the nation to file to join an inmate lawsuit against a state. Our strategic foundation was disruption of business as usual. We not only meant to disrupt the provision of services, but also to pressure policy-makers and political leaders to hold bureaucrats accountable. So we marched on state offices, bosses' offices, sat in at or took over the offices of state bureaucrats who were unresponsive, unaccountable, even on making dangerous decisions. The workers won pay raises and obtained much better working conditions.

Our legal effort with corrections officers and employees shocked and scared the state government. Prisons are all about them and us. Even though our motion to join the inmate lawsuit was kicked out, we won. When we said officially the prison in Alto wasn't working, that it was too violent, short-staffed, and over-populated, the whole state apparatus was shocked. We got a warden transferred and two hundred additional corrections officers hired.

This kind of strategic thinking and bold action characterized the Georgia State Employees Union Local 1985 of SEIU. We like to say we built that union on wit and grit. And that's the truth.

We organized at the state's mental hospitals as well. We put together a program that could wield and exercise the power we were building. We decided to exercise our power through militancy, through politics and legislation, and through the law. We hired young attorneys just out of law school to represent our members in disciplinary cases. We built a culture of militancy with marches and office takeovers to force bargaining on specific issues. We developed a statewide political machine to be able to win legislatively, especially in rural areas where state hospitals and prisons are typically built. By the time Andrew Young ran for governor in 1990, the *Atlanta Journal Constitution* called us "the powerful statewide union running his field operation."

One day a year we combined all the elements of power into a grassroots lobby day. Busloads of state employees pulled up to the State Capitol in the middle of the legislative session. So many workers filled the Capitol, all of them asking to see their state representatives and state senators that legislative business ground to a halt and the chambers adjourned early. We won pay raises, health and safety standards, improvements in working conditions, sick leave, dues check off, and we stopped privatization and short staffing. Seven years after its formation, 7000 workers were members of SEIU Local 1985.

At that point, I was asked to run for President of the Atlanta AFL-CIO. The challenge of organizing the 1996 Atlanta Olympics lay before me.

5

The Olympic Challenge

WHEN ATLANTA'S African-American-led unions and
the progressive white-led unions realized they constituted
an electoral majority of delegates on the labor council
and that this would allow them to elect the officers they
wanted, they asked me to run for president of the Atlanta
AFL-CIO. I was elected early in 1991. Our ultimate
goal was to take on the task of organizing the upcoming Olympics, but we were by no means strong enough
yet. The building trades couldn't so much as get a serious
meeting with the Olympics managing committee. I came
into office consumed with power, talking about it, knowing that to build power we had to organize and grow. We
had to be tough and strategic about building and wield-
ing power. We had to work united with community, civil
rights, and faith organizations on issues of justice. We had
to embrace and support African-American political power.

In short, we had to see our labor movement as part of a broader effort to build a social movement.

In the months before our bid for making the Olympics union, there were times of conflict, times of irony, and even times of comedy. An outraged call came in from a building trades business agent the day after a march for health care. His local had been lined up to march next to Atlanta Pride. Horror of horrors! Mostly, however, I recall many inspiring moments of solidarity. One hundred members of other unions showed up to lobby the city council for a raise for the American Federation of State, County, and Municipal Employees (AFSCME) union members who weren't even present. Another time, many of us straight trade unionists marched outside Cracker Barrel with our LGBT brothers and sisters chanting, "We're here. We're queer. Get used to it!" There was a beautiful campaign we waged with the civil rights and faith community to maintain free prescription drugs for homeless and indigent people at Grady Hospital. At one point in that campaign, 200 of us disrupted a Dekalb County Commission meeting by singing, "This Little Light of Mine."

We learned the lessons of movement civil disobedience from those who had worked closely with Dr. King: Reverend James Orange, Dr. Joseph Lowery, Andrew Young, and the Reverend Jesse Jackson. We learned politics and about political power from Black pioneers of political power like Maynard Jackson, Andrew Young, and John Lewis as we worked on their political campaigns. We worked at militancy. We were able and willing to disrupt business as usual, to engage in nonviolent direct action, to march and rally and raise hell and demonstrate in ways that not only made our enemies uncomfortable, but also kept them from carrying on business as usual, even costing them money, and eroding business as usual.

To that end, at a rally I'll describe in more detail later on, a thousand of us took over the K-Mart in the nicest part of Atlanta. Our sit-in effectively shut down the store and pressured the corporation to bargain in good faith and negotiate a first contract at their massive distribution center and warehouse in North Carolina.

In another example, Jobs With Justice (JWJ), a committee of our labor council, served as our solidarity arm, lending support to organizing campaigns, strikes, and community struggles. Similar to our action at K-Mart, our JWJ committee took over newspaper offices in Macon and Columbus and an Atlanta TV station in support of the Detroit newspaper strike against Gannett and Knight-Ridder.

But our labor movement, our fledging social movement, and our coalition taught us and the city of Atlanta the greatest lesson of all when we beat all the elements of

the Atlanta business and corporate community to unionize the 1996 Atlanta Olympics.

As we started planning our campaign to unionize the
Olympics, we knew victory would require use of every
available source to power and every avenue of militancy,
a broad coalition, political juice, and as close to a perfect
campaign as we could run. We began by meeting with the
Olympic Chief Operating Officer A.D. Frazier. He told
us this would be the first completely privately financed
Olympics and that they would do all the work as cheaply
as they could. In response, we proposed a city council
resolution calling for work on the Olympics to be done at
prevailing wages, to include training, health insurance,
and pensions, and to be done with the utmost concern for
safety. Both the city council and Mayor Maynard Jackson
supported the resolutions. Because of his values, Mayor
Jackson was supportive of organized labor on principle.
Most of the city council shared his values. Moreover, most
residents of most big cities are workers and many are union
members. Mayor Jackson repeatedly said the work on the
Olympics must be done union. Then we methodically began
meeting with organizations and leaders to build support.

In March of 1992 we found out the Olympic flag
would begin flying over the city the following September.
Immediately, we began planning and mobilizing for the
largest demonstration in the city's history. Every Friday

morning our building trades and Jobs With Justice committee met jointly to plan the action and build the turnout with the assistance of Rev. James Orange.

On September 18, 1992, we put 10,000 people led by the Rev. Jesse Jackson on the streets of Atlanta, effectively overwhelming the Olympic flag ceremony. The *Journal Constitution* called the march "spirited," to say the least. Our 10,000 came from every union, especially the building trades and from every functioning community and civil rights organization in the town. We carried signs proclaiming, "Unions built Atlanta, why not the Olympics?" Some unions even bused activists in from other towns and cities in Georgia and, in some cases, neighboring states. As Rev. Jackson said so clearly, "It's not merely an economic struggle, it's a moral struggle."

A few months later we met with our community allies in an all-day meeting to come up with a Christmas "wish list" for the 1996 Atlanta Olympics. Thanks to all of the effort that had come before, the list was not one of separate community and labor demands, but a single document with a single list of demands.

Three days before Christmas in 1992, eighty disciplined union leaders and staff and twenty equally tough community leaders succeeded in taking over Olympic headquarters to deliver our Christmas list. They were able to force a two-hour meeting on what the 1996 Olympics meant for the workers and average people of Atlanta. At the same time I was in Mayor Jackson's office attending a meeting on the same subject. The next day I got a call from the Executive Vice President for External Affairs of the Olympic Governing Board, Shirley Franklin (who went on to become a two-term mayor of Atlanta). She said they wanted a meeting the next week and they wanted the meeting at night in my office. So, we met secretly in my office at night in order to have as honest and off-the-record meeting as possible.

Shirley arrived at my AFL-CIO office in the International Brotherhood of Electrical Workers building at the appointed date and time. She brought a silk-stocking lawyer with her.

After the niceties, how was your Christmas, and so on, the lawyer looked at me and said, "Stewart, I've been in this work for 25 years involved in labor and civil rights issues (he didn't mention always on the company side), and we know that last action got out of hand. It didn't go the way you meant for it to. I've never seen a group of folks take over someone else's space like that."

I looked at Shirley and said, "We've been telling you that we will do whatever it takes short of hurting someone to make sure the work on the Olympics is done righteous." Righteous meant with fairness, adhering to the principles of justice and the common good.

To which the lawyer said, "Does that mean breaking the law?"

"Of course it does, Lloyd," responded Shirley. Then the future mayor leaned forward, rested her arms on her side of my desk, looked me straight in the eye and said, "Stewart, when rich white men get scared, I get scared. And rich, white men are scared."

I responded that maintaining the status quo was not an option. Union density and market share and wages were either going to increase because of the size of the project or they were going to decrease. The meeting ended with me wondering when they would call back for a more substantive pressing of the issues. They never did.

We continued with our coalition work, deepening it especially with Concerned Black Clergy. My pastor, Rev. Tim McDonald of First Iconium Church, was chairman. We grounded all our Olympics work in the larger community labor coalition. We also began preparing for the 1993 mayor's race. We decided to endorse city councilman Bill Campbell who was controversial, young, and unknown. The business community and Ambassador Andy Young and some of the civil rights leaders supported Fulton County Commission Chairman Michael Lomax. The county, however, had done $900 million of building non-union. Lomax was a non-starter, as far as we were concerned. Campbell was our candidate.

In about March of 1993, the Olympic leadership announced that they would break ground on the new centennial Olympic Stadium on July 10. Much fanfare and civil celebration were called for. Rev. McDonald convened our coalition. We agreed to erect a tent city two months before ground breaking on the very site where the new stadium would be built. We also decided to disrupt the ground breaking if we didn't have an agreement on construction of the stadium. And so we did. On most nights, forty to fifty community leaders, activists, and even homeless people slept on the site. Shirley Franklin brought soup because she is a decent and progressive woman. We had raised so much hell against the Olympic Committee that they didn't want it to appear as though they weren't interested in the community or workers.

Every night I slept on a cot under an Army tent with the side flaps raised. By mid-May the drama was building. About two weeks before the ground breaking, every local newscast included a live shot from tent city with me and others demanding the Olympics be done righteous or there would be no groundbreaking and no Olympics.

Finally, on a Thursday night, two nights before the Olympic Stadium groundbreaking, Rev. James Orange, Charlie Key of the building trades, and I met in our tent city and came up with a strategy to take over the ceremony. As president of the Atlanta AFL-CIO, I knew the

Left: Acuff presents Mayor Maynard Jackson an award for supporting Union Olympics.

Right: Acuff with Mayor Jackson as he accepts award from the Atlanta AFL-CIO.

city budget well. I knew how many police officers the city had and how many they could deploy to this event. We had already called for a demonstration on the morning of the ground breaking. We knew it would draw thousands of our members and allies. The plan we hit upon that Thursday night would send fifty people at a time over the bicycle barricades. We felt sure that when a couple hundred of our folks broke through, the police presence would be exhausted. Then we would simply take the stage and the microphone and turn the ground breaking into a rally for a just Olympics.

About 11:00 that same night when Shirley Franklin arrived with soup for all of us, the Rev. Orange and I pulled her off to the side. "Shirley," I said, "everything we said we would do, we've done. Now, I'm telling you that if we don't have an agreement on the stadium by Saturday morning, there won't be a groundbreaking ceremony. Tonight we figured out exactly how to disrupt the ceremony and take it over."

Shirley said she'd make some calls right away. The building trades went into bargaining first thing Friday morning and by 6:30 Friday evening there was an agreement on the construction of the Centennial Olympic Stadium. The news Saturday morning about the ground

Acuff introduces Ambassador Andrew Young announcing breakthrough agreement on Olympic Stadium.

breaking was full of the historic agreement reached the day before. Nonetheless, 1000 of our members and allies showed up for the pre-planned rally, only now it was a rally of unbridled celebration. Ambassador Young and Olympic Chief Operating Officer A.D. Frazier joined us. I was so overjoyed that I introduced Frazier, the target of our campaign, as my new good friend.

We were over the hump, but we were a very long way from done. There are thousands of different jobs involved in staging the Olympic Games. We had broken the arrogance of the Atlanta Olympic Governing Body. Work on the iconic and signature venue was guaranteed to be righteous. Another thirty venues would need to be either constructed or renovated or changed to accommodate Olympic sports. So we got busy on Bill Campbell's campaign against Lomax, doing all we legally could to help him win the November election.

We were successful. The night of his victory party, Campbell asked me to stand with his family. After he thanked his family, he thanked both organized labor and me, memorably declaring, "There ain't no labor like organized labor." I was happy to work on his inauguration day. Instead of the usual corporate and political bigwig events, we held a prayer service followed by a march to Dr. King's tomb, the county hospital, poor neighborhoods, and the State Capitol, winding up at City Hall.

When the new Mayor Campbell showed up at the January Atlanta A FL - C I O meeting, he had the city beat press corps in tow along with his two young children. I introduced him almost as soon as he walked in. Mayor Campbell didn't speak long. But he spoke very powerfully to those warriors for justice. "I wouldn't be mayor tonight without him, and that's why tonight I am announcing that I'm appointing Stewart Acuff as my representative to the Olympic Governing Board." Everyone jumped to their feet at once, yelling and screaming, feeling the way that only comes when average folks unite in collective power and struggle mightily for justice and for victory.

The activists in that room had organized and demonstrated for months to make sure the Olympics would be done righteous. They had worked hard to elect Bill Campbell. We had won a huge victory on the construction of the stadium. With my appointment by the mayor, we all knew our fight to make the Olympics righteous would turn from struggle to negotiation. We recognized that the mayor had legitimized and validated the power of our labor movement.

6

The "Controversial Speaker of the House"

THE MEETINGS of the Olympic Governing Body were strange for me, the street level organizer. It really was a trip from the streets to the suites. My new position was evidence of the power organized labor and workers had built and wielded in Atlanta. Not every job could be union because it was only a three-week event. In spite of that constraint, every job was done at union wage rates. Indeed, during one dispute about construction work, the Olympics construction manager told me that every job they *could*, they *would* do union.

Meanwhile, the nation had suffered a Republican tsunami in the 1994 elections. Newt Gingrich and his work on the conservative agenda in the "Contract with America" cast a long shadow. Although Gingrich had won in a suburban district, we in the Atlanta labor movement took his victory very hard. In January of 1995, we

began planning one of our most militant actions ever. We
would take over Gingrich's Congressional District Office.
Compared to other members' offices, it was large, with
two floors, two conference rooms, and a warren of staff
cubicles. I knew there would be massive blowback, so I
processed the action thoroughly. I sent out a memo to
leaders and activists about it. We discussed it openly at
the February 1995 Atlanta AFL-CIO meeting. I sought
the guidance of many, including Wade Rathke, because
as leader and chief organizer of ACORN, he'd organized
hundreds of militant actions.

Then, on March 15, 1995, we did it. We began with a
preparatory meeting at the IBEW hall, part direct action
planning, part prayer meeting. The Rev. Orange lead us in
prayer. This would be a nonviolent but militant action to
show America that ordinary Americans, average, working
Americans where Gingrich lived, didn't support him, his
agenda, or his contract. Two hundred of us rolled out in
four chartered buses to his district headquarters in Cobb
County. Once there, we stormed his office, chanting and
singing, "We Shall Not Be Moved," over and over.

When the police came, we started to leave. I was to
be the last out of the building to make sure no one was
arrested after I left. All was going as smoothly as could
be expected until the brass got there. The Cobb County
police major had his men detain me and take me to a

conference room. He demanded I identify some of the folks that he said had committed battery. I refused, telling him I had planned the action, was responsible, and that the arrests should start with me. Outside, Rev. James Orange noticed I was missing and suggested the crowd go back in and get me out. I asked the major to hold off on my arrest until I could go outside, quiet the crowd, and get them on the buses. Instead, they let me go and arrested Rev. Orange and another African American. It was clear to all the activists that while the police didn't arrest me, they did arrest the only two African-Americans present because of racism. It took us all day to get them out of jail.

What a storm ensued! The pre-Fox-News Sean Hannity, just a radio loudmouth in those days, came out with his trusty tape recorder. Radio host Laura Ingraham had me on her show. Rush Limbaugh talked about the action. The *Atlanta Journal Constitution*'s Rich Greer, who later would become the Laborers Union (LIUNA) communications director, wrote a full-page story about the action in which he thoroughly explained our grievances with Gingrich. Death threats poured in. Gingrich threatened to prosecute us. We got just as much attention from the other side. Progressives across America conveyed words of support and appreciation for taking on Gingrich in such a powerful way. Just a few weeks later, longtime friend and ally, Fred Azcarate, director of Jobs With Justice, asked me to speak about the action and militancy at their annual meeting. After that speech, progressives and unionists began to demonstrate at Gingrich book events and at the offices of his Congressional supporters. By the summer of 1995, Gingrich was the "controversial Speaker of the House."

As we kept the heat on with three more actions in Atlanta and many more actions around the nation, I attracted my own intelligence officers. One hailed from the Atlanta police. He and I had a cordial check in every week. The other was from the federal government, most likely the FBI. In the fall of 1995, Gingrich was forced to resign. If there ever was a lesson that direct action of my community organizing experience and the militancy of trade unionism worked, the downfall of Gingrich was that lesson.

During our fight against Gingrich, John Sweeney, Rich Trumka, and Linda Chavez-Thompson waged their campaigns for President, Secretary-Treasurer, and Executive Vice President of the National AFL-CIO. They ran as reformers who sought to emphasize and create more organizing. Their goal was to make the labor movement more powerful. They also vowed to reach out and build support amongst natural, progressive allies as we had done in Atlanta.

I was the first local AFL-CIO officer to publicly declare support for them. I also worked with SEIU organizer Andy Levin to build support across the AFL-CIO's 600 state and local central bodies. I couldn't have been more active in their campaign. Andy Levin and I worked assertively to build a grassroots network of local institutional support for Sweeney and his running mates. We succeeded.

I had been so outspoken that by the time we got to the October 1995 convention in New York City, I was asked to play a special role in the election and convention. On Sunday, the day before the convention opened, I debated the current president of the AFL-CIO, Tom Donahue, on a national broadcast. As one of the senior elected AFL-CIO officials who supported Sweeney, Trumka, and Chavez-Thompson solidly, I helped coordinate a meeting of state and local AFL-CIO affiliates. And that Sunday night, I emceed the last Sweeney, Trumka, and Chavez-Thompson rally of the campaign. By the end of the week, AFL-CIO had leadership more open to the outside, much more focused on organizing, and dedicated to turning state and local AFL-CIO chapters into mobilization structures.

7

Sierra Leone

AS I WRITE this chapter, I'm sitting in the airport of
Cartajena, Colombia, waiting to go home after a meeting
of global western hemisphere public sector unions. The
sights, sounds, and feelings of another tropical country
on the other side of the Atlantic are vivid in my thoughts.
I'm back in 1996 when my relationship with Ambassador
Andrew Young offered a once-in-a-lifetime opportunity.
Young's African-American Institute was helping to recruit
U.N. observers for the first democratic election in Sierra
Leone, then the fourth poorest country in the world. At
the time, Sierra Leone was in the middle of what some
called a civil war and others said was an all-out siege by
bandits. I was looking for a new challenge. Signing on as
an election observer in Sierra Leone qualified.

After a long, exhausting flight, including a three-hour
layover in Amsterdam, we landed at the airport of Sierra

Leone's capital city, Freetown. It was my first real taste of the tropical developing world. The airport was on an island. To get to our hotel in Freetown we had to board ancient Russian helicopters. The story was that these helicopters and their pilots had once been part of the Russian military assigned to provide assistance to Libya. But years earlier, the pilots had simply flown them away from Libya and the Russian military to establish their own transport business in Sierra Leone.

Although I was no stranger to air travel, nothing in my experience could have prepared me for the shock of boarding a military helicopter and throwing my luggage in the middle. There were no safety briefings, no seat belt instruction, and definitely no beverage service. The machine shook violently and took off oh-so-slowly. Somehow, we made it to the mainland in one piece and were taken to our beachfront hotel. Following some free time to adjust to the jet lag, we had many briefings, especially by the American Ambassador and the Embassy's military attaché. During those briefings, we were warned against trusting the military and taught to always seek out a non-governmental organization, or NGO, with a satellite phone in case of a bandit attack. We were constantly reminded that the country was unstable, totally unfamiliar with democracy and voting, and that its infrastructure was a mess.

I told my team leaders that I had never been to Africa and might never get back. I asked to be sent to the most remote site possible. They complied with an assignment to a town called Bo. I was part of a group of eleven that included folks from the United Nations, the British High Commission on Human Rights, the World Council of Churches, and those of us from the African-American Institute. We landed at an airport with a grass airstrip.

Bo was hotter, dustier, and more humid than anything I'd ever experienced. It had dirt streets, few automobiles, and crushing poverty. The air was heavy with the smoke of hundreds of wood and charcoal cooking fires. For a while, we ate wonderfully delicious bananas and chicken with French fries until air deliveries stopped due to the proximity of the rebels. After that we ate cassava root, a traditional African staple topped with gravy and goat meat.

The municipal electric system provided power only six hours a day. Our hotel, an ancient two-story colonial constructed building, had none of the amenities Westerners are used to, save indoor plumbing and private bathrooms. Fortunately, it was located in the town square just next to an upstairs open air bar that, for some reason I will never understand, played the American country-western singer Don Williams most of the time. I apparently drank all of the liquor in town, a double shot of scotch and a double of

British gin. Did I say the hotel had no air conditioning? We were in Bo for two weeks and I don't remember air conditioning ever.

We began our work straightaway. First we reached out to the NGO Doctors Without Borders to get the lay of the land. We also made arrangements to use their satellite phone in an emergency. They were gracious and friendly. They wanted to know what kind of aircraft would be sent to evacuate us, if necessary. Fixed-wing, we replied. World-wise and experienced in providing services in the middle of wars, rebellions, and revolutions, they informed us that a fixed-wing aircraft would be useless because it required an airport. During a potential bandit attack, the airstrip would be the most vulnerable and dangerous place in town. After learning this disturbing information, we next met with the police chief. He was a mountain of a man, at least 6′5″ and 275 to 300 pounds, who promised as much protection as he could muster during the bandit attack he thought likely because of the upcoming elections.

But the chief was very honest. "I can't guarantee your safety with our town surrounded by brutal rebels and a corrupt army," he stressed. In every discussion and encounter, we were reminded of the proximity of the rebels and their brutality. All day, every day, I felt both high and low levels of adrenaline flowing through my body.

Even though the townspeople and their leaders spoke with either fear or resignation about the civil war, almost all were excited about the possibility of democracy, elections, and freedom.

Our work included everything related to the elections: trainings on voting, speaking at the rallies of more than a dozen political parties, meeting with election officials, the mayor, town elders, teachers, and trade unionists. We taught people to set up voting booths and how to cast ballots. We spoke as neutrals at political rallies, reiterating the support of the international community. We walked refugee camps housing as many as 7000 people and urged them to vote. We met with union leaders and other community leaders. We had extensive discussions with the mayor and trained her staff on holding elections.

Victims of bandit attacks populated many camps. There we learned about Komandoes, traditional hunters whose weapons were old, single-shot and double-barreled shotguns. The Komandoes lived in the jungle and protected Bo from attacks. Everyone believed that Komandoes were invulnerable to bullets and knives. They would be able to protect the polling places from the rebels who were waging a campaign of terror throughout the countryside. The rebels would mercilessly hack off hands and arms with machetes because, as they declared, "How can you vote with no hands?"

After two weeks of doing almost everything imaginable connected to an election, it was Sunday morning, the day before balloting began on Monday and Tuesday. While in Sierra Leone, I had stopped working out. Even though I've always been an avid runner and fitness junkie, I just couldn't bring myself to burn energy that way when most of those around me couldn't get enough calories. I got up very early on that day and made an exception. I decided to go for a run. As I ran toward the edge of town, I started seeing people running in the opposite direction. After several minutes, I finally asked someone what was going on. "The rebels have attacked the town!" Feeling very foolish, I ran back to the hotel. People full of fear and bewilderment filled the streets. Young people, teenagers, ran by with crude weapons. They carried hoes and other primitive agricultural implements while chanting and singing, "We go to the fight!" The town calmed as dusk began to descend.

Monday began with the same commotion as Sunday. Still, we saw people determined to vote. Komandoes with ancient shotguns protected the interminable lines. I will always remember thinking, "How will these traditional hunters, no matter how brave, protect this polling place if it is attacked by bandits carrying rocket-propelled grenade launchers and AK-47's?" I don't know how, but somehow the Komandoes succeeded.

By midday, we observers went back to the hotel for our safety. The streets were jammed with people. From the roof of the hotel, we watched in horror as a crowd beat and stoned a man to death. His dead body was then quartered, one appendage at a time. Some of the attackers brandished his severed head on a pole while others set to completely disemboweling the body. All that remained was his limbless, headless trunk. A couple of hours later we saw another crowd drag a flayed body through the streets. In both cases, our friends told us the victims were rebels who had tried to disrupt voting. Despite all the chaos, by the end of the first day of voting many had cast ballots.

Early the next morning we awakened to two uniformed soldiers stumbling drunkenly down the street, weapons drawn and at the ready, shouting, "You say I'm a rebel, I kill you. Come say to my face. Say I'm a rebel. I will kill you." It was rumored that the army tolerated the rebels and that some behaved as rebels at night and soldiers by day. The locals even had a name for them: "so-bels." As our team gathered and talked about our day, we decided it wasn't safe to stay. We went to the post office with the one workable phone in town. It was no longer working. While we had all been doing election work, Prakash, an ethnic Hindi in our party, had planned for this day. He had a friendly connection with the matriarch of the Lebanese merchant community, so when we went to her house and asked to use the phone, she said, "Of course."

Prakash then called his United Nations contact who instructed him to bribe the army into securing the airfield. Then he was to call them back, and they would send a plane. I will never forget listening to Prakash call the Army Colonel.

"Colonel, this is Prakash with the United Nations, part of our election observer team in Bo." His voice rose at least an octave to a very non-threatening high, soft pitch. "Thank you for your great work securing the town and people of Bo. The election is going very well. Our work here is done. It is time for us to go back to Freetown and write our report that the election has been a great success here in Bo."

Silence while the Colonel responded.

Prakash then said, "We are calling to ask that you secure the airfield so we can go back to Freetown and write our excellent report. Of course we know there are costs associated with such a task. There will be fuel for your equipment, food for your men and other things. How much will you need?"

One hundred dollars was the reply. The Colonel said to leave it with the Lebanese matriarch. It was the most valuable one hundred dollars ever. Prakash called the U.N. back. They told us to call the police and ask them to send vehicles to the hotel with armed police officers. They also told us to get our team packed quickly and checked out of the hotel. We were to wait together till we heard or saw the plane, then go to the airport with the police. Prakash and I walked briskly back to the hotel. Running would have attracted too much attention. We shared the news with our team. Everyone was soon waiting in the lobby.

Waiting during a crisis or dangerous situation is not like waiting when you are bored. It is a time of hope and despair, of guessing and wondering. When will they come to get us? Will the army turn on us? Will the rebels attack us? One of the young women in our group said, "We're going to die today." I tried to reassure her: "We will both die, but not today. Neither of us will die today." Finally, we heard the plane. Rushing outside, the eleven of us jammed ourselves, including all our gear, into four police vehicles. Police officers with automatic machine guns hung out of the windows as we raced to the airport.

Halleluiah! Fifty to one hundred uniformed soldiers had stationed themselves around the landing strip and on the tiny, disused flight control tower. It was a civilian plane, but four heavily armed men got out to hustle us with our luggage aboard. As we took off, I turned to one of the team and asked, "How high do we have to be to be beyond small arms fire?" After we were certain we were out of danger, it was the most joyous, relaxing, and happy plane trip of my life. A very worried and grateful U.S. Ambassador greeted us when we landed and held a gala reception for us at his home that night.

I remember just wanting to relax and enjoy life. I spent a lot of time on the beach and in the water the next few days. One day I helped a group of fisherman from Guinea haul in their nets. I visited the beach bars. We went into Freetown. I bought small woven baskets just like the Geechee people on Sea Island off Georgia still make. I savored my life and the adventure until it was time to go home.

In Africa, I learned that life is sweet, that you can be calm in a dangerous situation, and that every day matters. My experience also showed me so clearly that democracy is not a natural human state. Democracy must be learned, sometimes with great difficulty. I saw firsthand how difficult it is to hold elections in a country beset by civil war. Today, I wish George W. Bush had known as much before he misled us into two wars in the Middle East.

In my own way, I fell in love with the country of Sierra Leone and its people. Partly it was that my time there was always exciting and adrenaline never stopped flowing through my veins. Mostly, though, it was a strange sense of kinship. The forebears of the people I met in Sierra Leone had been captured for the slave trade. Those slaves, the distant relatives of the courageous people risking their lives to vote, were also the distant relatives of many Americans with African blood. I am one of those people.

Bo and Sierra Leone had a profound effect on me. Had it not been for the prospects of a new national AFL-CIO leadership and a more aggressive labor movement, the rest of this book would be the story of a man working in the developing world.

8

Strike

POWER IS never given to people. They must take it. Many times, strikes are an important part of the process of taking power away from the elite and putting it where it belongs, with working people.

In 1996, the unionized staff of Detroit's two major newspapers, the *Free Press* and the *News* went on strike. The Atlanta AFL-CIO hosted road warriors from Detroit to pressure other Gannett and Knight-Ridder media outlets. We met with board members in Atlanta and picketed the newspaper in Gainesville, Georgia. We turned up the heat in Macon when 100 of us took over the lobby of the *Macon Telegraph*. By now the two newspaper conglomerates had figured something was going on in Georgia. They hired security. Because of that, we had a more hostile reception when we tried to take over the newspaper office in Columbus, Georgia.

We planned our action in Columbus on a Friday afternoon, just two weeks after I had broken my right arm in a car crash. The doctor had put two pins in it, wrapped it in a soft cast, and hung it in a sleeve. The police acted quickly and with grim determination. To make sure I was compliant, the Columbus Police Sergeant grabbed my broken arm when he arrested me. I soon found myself sitting in the bare concrete holding cell of the Muscogee County Stockade, thinking about the Merle Haggard song about that very jail. I wondered if I would spend the weekend there. I asked a jailer for some ibuprofen because my arm hurt so much. He brought down the nurse who looked at my arm, felt it, and said, "He don't need nuthin'. If it hurts it'll keep him from fightin'." Fortunately, my friends and colleagues bailed me out later that afternoon. The dinner of fried chicken and French fries on the way back to Atlanta was one of the best meals of my life.

There's a lesson here. Just because we've become used to nonviolent civil disobedience, you should never assume that both police and protesters understand and follow unwritten rules. If you anger the wrong person, you're just another criminal.

Strikes on a much larger scale helped us force the United Parcel Service to back off from shifting workers from full-time, full-benefit positions to part time work. The Teamsters wisely latched onto that issue knowing it

Upper photo: Acuff and Muscogee County police officer in Columbus, GA, during protest opposing companies owning the Detroit newspapers.

Lower photo: Acuff on the way to the Muscogee County stockade.

would resonate with the American people. And they were right. Americans were sick of contracting out, outsourcing, offshoring, and part-timing work in America. The Teamsters called a national strike. Because the headquarters of UPS is in Atlanta, our labor movement immediately became a focus of activity.

To help us turn up the heat, the AFL-CIO sent one its best organizers and trade unionists, former United Mineworkers organizer John Cox. John was the calm in the storm, the one who made everyone comfortable. He could make the most difficult meeting easy. He knew how to make others laugh and he knew when to do it. He seemed so easy-going, even when he was working like mad to get things done. You always wanted to be around him. But more than anything, John had the greatest sense of values I have ever seen in an organizer. He loved workers and average people and he hated injustice. Love workers. Hate injustice. John Cox was a source of strength in the days ahead.

As soon as the strike was called, the Atlanta AFL-CIO called a demonstration of 300 activists from other unions in a show of solidarity with the Teamsters. Those striking at UPS were not alone. We rallied on picket lines. We walked picket. The Airline Pilots Association refused to haul "struck" freight. The entire Atlanta labor movement stepped up and stepped out.

For the next thirteen days, I spent twelve to sixteen hours a day with John. We worked hip-to-hip all day, every day. We organized picket line rallies together and boosted the flagging spirits of strikers. Then we began to organize the event that would convince UPS management they were not going to win this one. Soon, 4000 people demonstrated in front of the UPS facility in Pleasantdale, Georgia. Traffic backed up on I-85 for twenty-five miles. UPS settled the next day. The militancy of the Teamsters and the Atlanta labor movement was critical to the victory. Just as critical was the support of the general public. As it turned out, the men and women in brown had more political savvy than the management of Brown.

Strikes, however, can be a terrifying experience for workers. Most of us in America live paycheck to paycheck. During a strike there is no paycheck and no certainty that the next check will come. Furthermore, many of us in America have our self-image and sense of personal value tied to our work. When economic and psychological security come under threat, workers naturally and desperately want to get back on the job. Nonetheless, strikes can be successful when workers' sense of dignity and solidarity is more powerful than their fear of what walking out might mean to them and to their families.

9

A Page from Gandhi and Dr. King

NONVIOLENT civil disobedience means disobeying earthly law to better follow moral or heavenly law. It means sacrificing your freedom and comfort and convenience to protest and draw attention to injustice, to prick the conscience of the public, and to create a disruption to business as usual. Aggressive but peaceful and nonviolent civil disobedience can be remarkably successful. Nonviolent civil disobedience ended segregation and Jim Crow in the South. And nonviolent but aggressive civil disobedience helped us win many struggles in the Atlanta labor movement. We won important rights for K-Mart employees and kept medicines free for the homeless and indigent at Grady, a huge county charity hospital in Atlanta.

Nonviolent civil disobedience is central to the thinking of Mahatma Gandhi and Dr. Martin Luther King. Dr. King studied Gandhi in his preparation to head the modern day civil rights struggle. Many of us labor leaders and activists studied Gandhi's and Dr. King's ideas and actions at the King Center in Atlanta. We also learned much from the Southern Christian Leadership Conference, an organization rich with people who had worked directly with Dr. King as he marched and demonstrated against segregation and legalized racism throughout the South.

The Reverend Orange had been in Dr. King's inner circle. It was Rev. Orange who organized the high school students in Birmingham to leave school and face the dogs and fire hoses in the demonstrations that shook the collective conscience of America. Rev. Orange worked with gangs in Chicago during Operation Breadbasket and with gangs in Memphis during the AFSCME sanitation workers' strike. We worked with Rev. Orange, learned from him, and were inspired by him over and over.

When the Amalgamated Clothing and Textile Workers Union, ACTWU, organized the K-Mart distribution center in Greensboro, North Carolina, bargaining for the first contract was brutal and seemed fruitless. ACTWU kept busy across the South organizing private sector workers in spite of intense opposition from employers and the business community. An employer in Columbus, Georgia, actually hung and burned Southern Regional Director, Bruce Raynor, in effigy. It therefore came as no surprise that, in spite of the excellent campaign ACTWU had waged, K-Mart was determined to deny its workers a first contract on any collective bargaining agreement.

ACTWU took the fight for a first contract to Atlanta. Organizer Lane Windham came to see me and asked for the Atlanta labor movement to help stage a 1,000-person demonstration on the Saturday before Palm Sunday, one of the busiest shopping days of the year. She also asked that we get dozens of ministers and community leaders arrested in nonviolent civil disobedience. On the appointed Saturday, ACTWU bused in hundreds of activists to the IBEW Hall where they were joined by 200 to 300 Atlanta labor activists and community and religious leaders.

I met the week before with high-ranking officials from the police, corrections, and community affairs departments so that everyone would know what we were doing. We drove out to the K-Mart store in Buckhead, Atlanta's toniest neighborhood. The buses emptied in the parking lot and we staged a terrific rally with moving testimony from the workers who were fighting for a first contract. Then forty-one of us, concerned clergy, community, and union activists, walked into the store, chanting the whole time, and sat down. Talk about disrupting an important and big shopping day! The Atlanta police followed us in and one at a time put us under arrest, Bruce Raynor first.

They served us with citations and loaded us into a corrections bus bound for the city jail where we were released on our own recognizance. Two days later, K-Mart sent a new representative to the bargaining table and both sides agreed to a new contract by the end of the week.

Not all of our work was directly on behalf of workers' rights. We joined with community activists to oppose injustice wherever it might appear. We built strong support for our labor movement during our action against Grady Hospital. Grady, which had served Atlanta's poor for decades, suddenly announced it would no longer provide free medicines to the homeless and other indigent people. Organized labor's allies amongst homeless advocates and the Concerned Black Clergy began a campaign on behalf of those called by Jesus of Nazareth in Matthew 25, "the least of these." Even though the policy change did not directly affect union members, our commitment to our allies required that we join in their struggle.

I'd worshipped at the Rev. Tim McDonald's mostly African-American congregation at First Iconium Baptist Church every Sunday I could since 1990. "Rev. Mac" had a view of theology I thought was most true to the teaching of Jesus. I also loved the working class nature of the church, and I loved Rev. Mac and his wife and two kids. Working on the Grady campaign was therefore a joy. We spoke at meetings of Grady's Board of Directors and picketed Grady Hospital. Grady remained stubborn, so we turned to nonviolent, but aggressive, civil disobedience.

The City of Atlanta sits in two counties, Fulton and Dekalb. We decided to take over a monthly meeting of the Dekalb County Commission. There were about 200 of us protesters at this particular meeting. I'm proud to say that half of them were union activists. When the meeting began, Rev. McDonald began singing "This Little Light of Mine." All of us quickly joined in. The police were not long in coming and treated Rev. Mac pretty roughly. I went to him and was quickly put under arrest, somehow angering the arresting officer in the process. As I was being escorted to the police car, an officer grabbed me by the handcuffs and pulled up. I felt like my arms and shoulders would be dislocated. I cried out in pain, "I ain't fighting you, man! Ease up!" Ironically, one of Atlanta's TV stations captured that scene and ran it for a year in its advertisement for local news.

I was among the thirty union activists, clergy, and political leaders taken to the Dekalb County Jail. We were equally divided into three groups. I knew we wouldn't be long in jail. In short order, the sheriff came to our holding cell telling us we were free to go. Then state representative Douglas Dean said, "I can't go. We still haven't fixed the crisis for homeless and poor people at Grady." I said that if Doug Dean couldn't go, I couldn't go. If anyone was going to stay in jail, I was going to stay in jail. Altogether, ten of us chose to stay in jail. That, in itself, was local news.

The Sheriff put us in our own pod with about ten cells and an open, common area. We stayed up much of the night, imitating Paul and Silas in jail in the New Testament. We talked about Scripture and our values. We talked about nonviolent civil disobedience. We talked about our organizational relationships. Then we sang. We sang freedom songs and hymns, including all our favorite hymns. Finally, after midnight, we all retired to what in prison passes for a bed, that is, a steel cot, a thin pad, and a thin blanket. I got up at 5:30 the next morning to face a breakfast I would not wish on anyone.

Meanwhile, State Senator Vincent Fort took up the question of Grady, funding, and indigent medicines in a meeting with Governor Roy Barnes on the afternoon of our demonstration. In that meeting, Governor Barnes pledged millions of dollars from his discretionary fund to pay for indigent medicines at Grady Hospital. What a great victory!

At about ten in the morning we were released from jail. The entire local press corps was waiting for us. We had a combination victory rally and press conference in front of the jail. Total victory! We trade unionists had held up our end of the struggle in a serious effort at reciprocity. The campaign sealed our relationship with our most important and powerful allies.

10

The Battle of Seattle

THE WORLD TRADE Organization was to meet in Seattle, Washington, on November 30, 1999. Union activists across the world knew the rules to be discussed at the meeting would only benefit the elite of each country. We in the United States had watched manufacturing jobs disappear to other countries after the signing of NAFTA, the North America Free Trade Act. Manufacturing in Mexico also declined. Worse yet, NAFTA had required the Mexican government to end subsidies for growing corn and beans. Rising food prices and lower income for farmers in Mexico ravaged Mexican workers, leading to a spike in immigration from Mexico into the United States.

The Seattle AFL-CIO President, Ron Judd, and Western AFL-CIO Regional Directors, Mark Splain and Pat Lee, had been meeting with allies from the environmental and human rights community all up and down the West Coast. They were planning what came to be called the "Battle of Seattle." I volunteered to help with final planning and execution of the demonstration. I was detailed to John Sweeney, President of the AFL-CIO, whom I had known since he hired me in 1982. John was always easy, very humble, and by no means demanding. Still, when you're detailed like that, your job of personal assistant sometimes becomes that of bodyguard. I recall elbowing and pushing through huge crowds as I led John to the staging areas where he was to speak.

The demonstrations started on the night of November 29 when we encircled the King Dome during one of the many WTO events. The really big deal, however, was to occur the next day. The weather forecast called for periods of rain all day. We were up early to take our assigned places at a sports stadium where we expected 50,000 trade unionists. Plans called first for a rally, then for a march in the streets with our allies. I was assigned to the front line of labor's march. The rally was great but went on too long. There was so much excitement in the streets outside the stadium that folks began marching before the rally was over. I left the stadium and did all I could to keep the crowd from beginning the march without John Sweeney and all the union presidents. At long last, the rally ended and we led everyone to the front line and began the march.

Mark Splain from the AFL-CIO and I had to clear the street so the march could go through. The streets were full of demonstrators. People were everywhere, all kinds of people: union workers wearing their colors, young anti-globalization protestors, environmentalists, and lots of people who fit all these categories. More joined us as we marched steadily toward downtown Seattle. At some point I felt an invisible, but tangible, positive energy. The energy of tens of thousands of people of good will from different traditions, cultures, backgrounds, causes, and regions were united for global human rights, workers' rights, and environmental justice. The same energy radiated against corporate-fueled globalization, environmental degradation, poverty, and worker exploitation. Soon we were all swept up in a common joy.

Fifty thousand trade unionists marched through the streets of Seattle with tens of thousands of others demanding a better world and better lives for all humanity. That's the reason for all the talk of teamsters and turtles, of blue and green, referring to the solidarity of labor and environmentalists. For those of us who are organizers by trade, especially union organizers, all those lonely nights away from home in strange hotels in new cities or towns were redeemed, washed away by this massive sea of humanity moving in unity as an irresistible force. I could feel my sense of place in the world, my spiritual calling, and my understanding of who are my sisters and brothers broadening in ways that still serve me well. My hopes for what we could achieve began to grow.

After the march, I joined Mark Splain, Gerry Shea, also from the AFL-CIO, and other peacekeepers in retracing the route to look for union members who might have gotten separated. We had heard the police were to begin sweeping the streets to clear the crowds. As organizers typically do, we felt responsible for those who came out at our request. We came to one intersection and a young man with long red hair told us that no union people were there and that we should keep moving. Bristling as I often do when given an order, I relaxed and was grateful when he explained they expected a confrontation with the police in that intersection. He didn't have to do that, but people were looking out for each other in the Battle of Seattle. The young man knew what he was talking about. That night the police cut way back on arrests and began, instead, to shoot people with wooden dowels. They sprayed tear gas and used other non-lethal but very painful punishments. After that, downtown Seattle was declared "a no protest zone."

In spite of that, the next day the United Steelworkers Union called a demonstration on the docks to protest the practice of other countries dumping cheap steel in the American market. I joined people intent on marching into the no protest zone. Encouraged by the sound of makeshift drums beaten by young human rights protestors, we headed for the forbidden streets. When we got to the top of a hill near Pike's Place Market, we looked down the street and saw a large gathering of police in full riot gear. They marched to a cadence of three-foot-long riot batons tapping on their shin guards; we marched to the beat of drumsticks on upside-down pickle buckets. My heart, blood, and adrenaline were racing. I was sure I'd get the business end of one of those steel-reinforced batons. Instead, the police stopped at an intersection and blocked the three streets other than the one we were marching on. As we marched into the intersection, they let us have it with tear gas. They gassed us and gassed us. One of my friends, Teamster organizer Rob Hickey, was hit from behind with a gas canister that burned a hole in the back of his blue jeans. He kept those jeans for years. We were all coughing with tears streaming out of our eyes. The police unsealed one of the streets, then did the same thing at the next intersection and the next, deliberately not making arrests but doling out punishment to those in their way.

Those three days were glorious, joyous, painful, incredibly exciting, and enlightening. We won that battle. The World Trade Organization talks stalled. We weren't alone. We had broken down the barriers that separated unions from environmentalists. We had cemented our relationships with human rights groups and student activists. We created a major critique of unfettered corporate globalization. We were part of a power greater than any of us had ever experienced.

11

Politics and Organizing

JOE COSTIGAN, as much as anyone with whom I have
been privileged to work, understood the importance of
a strong political foundation in the struggle to convince
employers to accept the rights of workers to decide for
themselves whether or not they wanted a union. More
often than not, I have found that workers want to be in
a union. American labor law has been much too weak
to guarantee that freedom to workers. As I worked with
Joe, the seeds of what was to become the Employee Free
Choice Act, the EFCA, were being planted in my mind.

I became friends with Joe shortly after I was asked
in 2000 to take over the position of AFL-CIO's Deputy
Director of the Midwest Region Headquarters in
Chicago. I had already decided to leave Atlanta when the
right opportunity came along, so I jumped at the chance.
I'd never experienced anything like the Chicago labor

movement. It was huge, powerful, and established. My focus was to be organizing except during election season when everyone focused on politics. As things turned out, the country's political mood was turning hard right, and politics took most of my time.

During my time in Chicago, the Union of Needletrades, Industrial, and Textile Employees (UNITE) organized the mostly Latino workers in four commercial laundries. Joe was Political Director of the UNITE Midwest Joint Board during those campaigns. He was a master at using UNITE's political juice and, indeed, that of the whole labor movement, to win the freedom to form unions for workers trapped in poverty-level laundry jobs across Chicago. What I learned from him was important as my political work became all-consuming when Gore and Lieberman ran against Bush and Cheney. I was detailed to northern Wisconsin to do all we could to win that battleground state. We had a blast with Bruce Colburn and Scott Reynolds from the AFL-CIO phone banking, leafleting union worksites, and going door to door to union households. We carried Wisconsin for Gore and Lieberman, but only by about 5000 votes.

Then came the national recount. At the time, we were sitting-in at the office of the President of the University of Chicago. The University of Chicago Business School allowed union-busting law firms to use University facilities to conduct seminars. We were demanding that the practice be stopped. In came a call telling me that I had a plane ticket that night to Florida. When we finished the sit-in, I hustled home to pack for Florida. Then I was off to O'Hare to catch my flight. Within forty-eight hours of the disputed election, we had 200 of the best organizers and at least one hundred of the best labor lawyers in America assembled for the recount. Unfortunately, we didn't have a plan nor did we have the will and determination of those working on behalf of Bush and Cheney to win. While the Republican operatives were steadfast and militant, we were tentative, way too cautious, and timid.

The months leading up to the Supreme Court decision dragged on. There is no doubt that Gore and Lieberman won the 2000 national election. The Republican majority on the Supreme Court not only made a biased and terrible decision for Bush and Cheney, but also undermined the foundation of American democracy. Our last demonstration was at the State Capitol in Tallahassee while it snowed three feet on my wife and son back home in Evanston, Illinois. You can imagine how lonely and frustrated I felt.

The following year, the Oklahoma State Legislature introduced legislation to put "right to work" on the ballot. I was sent to Oklahoma to direct the efforts to defeat the legislation. Legislation that prevents a union and an employer from negotiating an all-union shop is misnamed "right to work." Private sector unions are required to represent all workers covered by their contract. We think everyone who benefits from a union contract and union representation should join the union. We didn't want Oklahoma to join the list of some twenty states with such flagrantly anti-union policies.

We got busy immediately in Oklahoma. I flew in on a Friday. The next morning, I met with the Democratic State Senate Leader. He purposely had assigned the legislation to the Commerce Committee instead of the Labor Committee. We knew the right-to-work legislation would come out of the Commerce Committee with a do-pass recommendation. We also knew the legislation would die in the Labor Committee. "What would it take to kill this legislation?" I asked him that Saturday morning in his small town Oklahoma law office. He was unmovable even though I described how a loss of union membership would hurt the Democratic Party. We lobbied the State Senate hard and flooded them with grassroots phone calls from union activists. In spite of our best efforts, the bill came out of committee and passed the State Senate. To this day I don't know if he favored right to work or not, but for some reason was unmovable.

While in Oklahoma I met many strong trade unionists like Tim O'Conner, president of the Oklahoma City

AFL-CIO, and Andy Frye of the Steelworkers. They, like
so many others, worked tirelessly to mobilize union members against "right to work." When the bill came out of the
Senate we pulled out all the stops to kill it in the House.
We traveled the state talking to union members, leaders of the Democratic Party, and activists and allies from
other groups who shared our values and politics. We held
a dinner for the Democratic Speaker of the House and
his leadership. There, and everywhere, we asked: "What
will it take to stop this legislation which will weaken both
labor and the Democratic Party?"

One day, Tim and I met with the entire Democratic
Caucus of the House of Representatives. "We, organized
labor and Democrats, have done so much together to make
work more noble and life less mean," I said to them. "Why
in the name of the Good Lord would you do anything
to weaken both our unions and the Democratic Party?"
No one ever had a good answer. I met with the labor
leadership almost daily looking for any way to stop the
legislation and to generate as much grassroots activity as
possible.

Finally, we began to mobilize for a major march on
the State Capitol the day before "right to work" was to
be voted on in the Oklahoma House of Representatives.
Three thousand union members and our allies turned out
for the largest march in Oklahoma's history. We filled the

streets all around the Oklahoma State Capitol, chanting, marching, and even serving up some tasty barbecue. Then we filled the hall of the capitol, buttonholing and lobbying members of the House, spilling into every corridor and crevice of the Capitol of the State whose motto is "Labor Vincit Omnia" or "Labor Over All."

I read a lot of Oklahoma history in those four months of commuting between Chicago to Oklahoma. I asked myself how a state that had once been so progressive and pro-union could have become so rightwing and anti-labor. Despite the largest and most consistent mobilization in Oklahoma history, the right to work legislation passed. There was only one thing left for me to do before I left Oklahoma. I needed to negotiate the date of the right to work referendum with the governor, Frank Keating, a rising star in the Republican Party.

To my surprise, we got a face-to-face meeting with him. Governor Keating was slim, fit, and had hair as white as cotton fresh from the boll. It was immediately clear that, just like Sarah Palin, his Republican Party popularity had as much to do with his looks as with his policies. We sat down in his office, each of us with a small entourage of three or four a piece. I've always thought Keating agreed to a face-to-face meeting as much out of curiosity as anything. Would I try to bribe him? Would I threaten him? Would I pound the table? What would I look like?

Indeed, what would a member of the AFL-CIO's national senior staff look and act like?

After the opening niceties, I said, "Governor, let's give the people of Oklahoma a real opportunity to decide this thing. Let's give this vote its own date. Let's have this vote on a day when nothing else is on the ballot." After going back and forth, he agreed. The vote would be on the third Tuesday in September 2001. I left Oklahoma. The AFL-CIO sent in a political team. Of course, everyone knows what happened in the weeks before the vote. The Twin Towers and the Pentagon were attacked on September 11. All the sudden, anti-unionism became synonymous with patriotism. The rightwing ads equated "right to work" with freedom. Despite getting three times as many votes as we thought we would need to win, we lost.

Fortunately, that's not the last of the story. After I was gone, the labor movement won collective bargaining for Oklahoma's public employees. Thousands of city and county state workers have organized and bargained for work that is nobler and life that is less mean. During the Bush years, every victory, no matter how large or small, was a major victory.

12

AFL-CIO Organizing Director

SOME PEOPLE work on the ground and others work in headquarters. For the most part, the two assignments are separate and require different skills. I was an exception, I guess. I moved on to Washington, D.C., still in my 40's, in the fall of 2001. The National AFL-CIO decided it needed a field team of organizers to mentor new affiliate union lead organizers to help run campaigns. They also needed someone to do hands-on training. They wanted to help affiliate unions run large, creative campaigns that had the potential in one way or another to affect the whole labor movement. They made me Deputy Organizing Director and Director of Field Operations to run this team.

Mark Splain and I were reunited, and we immediately began recruiting four Regional Organizing Coordinators. We successfully hired or transferred four great ones. We helped the Teamsters organize America West Airlines and got an organizing agreement for the Graphic Communications International Union at Quebecor Printing. We helped the Service Employees organize home care workers in Wisconsin and the International Federation of Professional and Technical Engineers in their nation-wide campaign at United Airlines.

A few months after I arrived in D.C., the organizing department of the AFL-CIO, led by Mark, proposed that the organization prioritize its efforts by economic sectors. At their summer meeting at the Drake Hotel in Chicago, the Executive Council agreed to the plan that would designate lead unions in each of eleven economic sectors. President Sweeney got so much negative feedback in the next few weeks, however, that we had to kill the plan. Splain, along with much of the leadership of the organizing department, left the AFL-CIO. After two weeks of vetting my name and my resume with national union presidents, President John Sweeney asked me to be the AFL-CIO Organizing Director. He wanted to put the AFL-CIO front and center in the conversation about organizing.

It's hard to describe what it was like for a lifelong organizer to become Organizing Director of the AFL-CIO. I could say it was the realization of a dream, but I'd never dreamed I'd rise to such a position. I could say I'd worked for it all my adult life, but I hadn't. My goal was simple in all those years: I always had worked to be the best organizer I could be and to be in the place I could do the most good and make the most happen. It's also hard to describe how rocky the road ahead of me was to be.

I became Organizing Director in October of 2002 during George Bush's first term. My entire time in the position would be served in the shadow of the most anti-union President since Herbert Hoover. To make matters worse, most of the senior staff who could have guided me had quit during the controversy that led to my appointment. And to top it all off, the AFL-CIO was beginning to fracture because the labor movement was shrinking and unable to grow. Though our shrinkage in absolute numbers was small, we were declining more rapidly as a percentage of the total work force. The Service Employees International Union, the Teamsters, the Laborers Union, the United Food and Commercial Workers, the Carpenters, UNITE HERE, and the United Farm Workers had formed a coalition called the New Unity Partnership. It was no secret they wanted to elect one of their own as president and take over the AFL-CIO.

The New Unity Partnership's idea for growth was to limit the organizing of national unions to the sector of the economy in which they had the most members. They would force small unions to merge into large unions.

The result would be a small number of very large unions concentrated in twelve to fifteen sectors of the American economy. Their plan never made very good sense as a growth strategy as far as I was concerned. Furthermore, it did not make a lot of sense as a way to consolidate power in the AFL-CIO and the American labor movement. The leadership of the AFL-CIO and the vast majority of presidents of national unions stood firmly against the plan.

Confining union organizing to core jurisdictions and forcing small unions to merge into big ones were terrible internal election planks in a platform to take over the AFL-CIO. The NUP failed to build support and eventually split from the AFL-CIO in a disastrous attempt to create a rival federation. But in the fall and winter of 2002-2003, that split was still two years away. I was focused on the overwhelming task of planning at the January 2003 AFL-CIO Organizing Summit that had been called before I was the director. I was determined to make it real and substantive.

Terese Bouey, from my ACORN days, and Bill Ragen were both seasoned organizers and assistant directors of the AFL-CIO organizing department. They worked long and hard with me to plan the Summit. Our goal was to organize the Summit around what the labor movement most needed to do in order to grow. We had sessions on resources and financing for organizing. We also had sessions on organizing outside the National Labor Relations Board. We did this because the National Labor Relations Act has been watered down since its passage in 1935. Today it doesn't provide effective penalties for violations. Employers can flaunt the rules with impunity. So we had sessions on how to work outside the NLRB to leverage employers to recognize workers' freedom to form unions and bargain collectively. My department's Organizing Institute also conducted sessions on the basic mechanics of organizing. Terese stayed up all night assigning the 250 attendees to those sessions we thought were most appropriate for each of them.

The Organizing Summit was a huge success. It got rave reviews from the attendees and the labor press. Most important among its outcomes was the realization and admission from organizers across the labor movement that workers in America had lost the right to organize and bargain collectively. We needed a national public policy fight and legislation to restore those freedoms. Larry Cohen, then the Organizing Director and Executive Vice President of the Communications Workers of America, CWA, and founder of Jobs With Justice, made that argument most clearly and articulately. Cohen set out American labor's biggest policy and legislative priority to this day: Give American workers the unfettered freedom to form unions and bargain collectively.

I remember being in the District of Columbia Hilton at the close of the Summit, sipping beer, sitting with one leg hooked over the arm of an easy chair as I gave an interview to the labor press. It was a very satisfying moment.

13

The Employee Free Choice Act

COMING OUT of the Organizing Summit we had a mandate to create legislation that would give workers in America greater freedom to form unions and bargain collectively. Unfortunately, not everyone saw or felt that mandate. Some of the desk jockeys at AFL-CIO didn't think legislation that included majority authorization or union recognition and certification based on workers signatures would "ever be taken seriously," or "pass the laugh test." Others couldn't agree on what should be included in the legislation. The task of convincing the staff bureaucracy of the AFL-CIO to introduce and fight for what was to become the Employee Free Choice Act (EFCA) fell to Andy Levin, assistant director of the Organizing Department, and me.

Andy came from one of Michigan's strongest political families. His uncle is Senator Carl Levin; his father is

Congressman Sander Levin. Andy's first month as a union organizer had been spent with me in East Texas back in the early 1980's. I had worked with him at the end of the first organizing campaign to make sure it was successful. And, of course, Andy and I had worked together on the ground and in field operations to elect John Sweeney President of the AFL-CIO.

Andy and I argued that the legislation should be narrow and focused on the most significant problems in organizing. It was by no means easy, but by the summer of 2003 we had agreement that the Employee Free Choice Act would include only three elements. First, it would allow workers to form a union by a majority simply signing a card to streamline the organizing process and limit the amount of time employers could intimidate or retaliate against workers. Second, it stiffened penalties against employers who violated the law. Third, it would allow workers to seek mediation and arbitration if they couldn't negotiate a first contract with their employer.

We asked veteran organizers Patti Devlin of the Laborers Union, Paul Booth of AFSCME, and Larry Cohen of the Communication Workers to present the policy to the AFL-CIO Executive Council. Massachusetts Senator Ted Kennedy and Congressman George Miller of California introduced the Employee Free Choice Act in November of 2003. As expected, Republicans, the

International Human Rights Day, 10 December 2003. Three thousand march in support of the Employee Free Choice Act.

business community, and other assorted critics scoffed at the idea. In response, we decided to do actions in as many media markets as possible on December 10, International Human Rights Day. The 1948 Universal Declaration of Human Rights, a global document adopted in the wake of the global struggle against Nazism, Fascism, and Japanese Imperialism, included the rights to form unions and bargain collectively. On that day in 2003, the rallies so many of our dedicated organizers worked so hard to plan and promote turned out about 150,000 people at 100 or so events across the country.

I was ecstatic. I traveled to as many of the events as possible, including one with Former Democratic

Congressional Leader David Bonior to the State Assembly chambers of Vermont. We packed the chambers of the General Assembly in Montpelier. Workers testified about the employer opposition they encountered when trying to organize. David Bonior talked about the need for a public policy solution and our legislation, the Employee Free Choice Act. I talked about growing inequality because of the destruction of the right to organize. I went back home to Atlanta where the Teamsters and the Atlanta AFL-CIO led half a dozen actions on one day, including a great rally at the notorious union-busting law firm, Jackson-Lewis. I went out to Portland, Oregon, where I spoke to 3000 unionists and allies before we marched through downtown streets led by Jobs With Justice and the Oregon State AFL-CIO.

Within weeks we had 100 co-sponsors for the EFCA in the U.S. House of Representatives. The legislation had passed the "laugh test." I hit the road hard and spoke everywhere I could get an invitation. We knew we'd never pass the Employee Free Choice Act with an "inside the beltway" strategy. We needed highly visible support all over America. My goal was, and still is as I write this, to create a social movement for passage of the Employee Free Choice Act.

President John Sweeney was pleased with my first year. There was much to be pleased about. There had been the 2003 Organizing Summit and the introduction of the EFCA. All the rallies in support of it had been a success, too. We were giving affiliates organizing assistance and the Organizing Institute was providing training. In addition, we'd gotten Congressional sign-ons to the Employee Free Choice Act. We had definitely put the AFL-CIO at the center of the organizing discussion. We had ongoing and regular meetings with national union organizing directors.

Throughout this period, I noticed that the leadership and staff of both AFL-CIO and national unions were coming to me for answers to thorny questions about union growth. I was also beginning to do more media work. I had always been the hell raiser, the ultimate field or street organizer. Now, I was supposed to have the answers to American labor's biggest problems. I was shocked and slightly intimidated when I made a speech in Chicago and read almost the entire transcript the next day in the Bureau of National Affairs Daily Labor Report.

Over the last several years I've probably written 100 blog posts, magazine articles, newspaper op-eds, and, now, two books. I've written almost every single word on airplanes somewhere between home and a speech I made, a workshop I conducted, or a high level meeting I attended. Bernie Pollack, a young activist who came to work for us after getting his master's degree at George Washington University and I knew that to build support for the Employee Free Choice Act, we had to move and mobilize the labor movement and the non-labor left. That meant speaking to every state AFL-CIO convention and metropolitan AFL-CIO, every union regional conference, and every organizing conference or national convention I could. That meant life on the road—"Crossroads will you ever let him go?" as Gregg Allman sang so beautifully in "Melissa."

Life on the road is exhausting, exhilarating, lonesome, boring, over-stimulating, and adrenaline pumping. You eventually fall into a routine: how you pack and what you take, what you do when you check in, how you triage your emails and phone calls, how you turn on the fan in a hotel's heating/cooling unit so you have white noise to cover up other noises, and even when and where you work out. For me, working out is critical to my physical and emotional health.

Of course, I have my favorite hotels around America. I like the Benson in Portland, the Crowne Plaza in downtown St. Louis, the Crowne Plaza overlooking the Mississippi River in St. Paul, the Holiday Inn in Duluth, the Drake in Chicago, the downtown Sheraton in Nashville, the downtown Doubletree in Memphis, and the downtown Doubletree in Little Rock. I have my favorite restaurants and watering holes, too, mostly kind of funky and casual. There's the Kitchen Express in Little

Rock, Sylvan Park and McCabe's Pub in Nashville, Jakes' Seafood in Portland, anywhere on the Hill in St. Louis, and all the bars and grills in all the Labor Temples across the Midwest and elsewhere like Missoula, Montana. Just writing the names of these places makes me happy. My two all-time favorites have to be Manuel's in Atlanta and T-Bone's Sports Grill in Chattanooga. During the 15 years I lived in Atlanta, I hung out at Manuel's with union folks, Democratic Party folks, journalists, cops, and anyone else who liked to kick back. President Jerry Lee of the Tennessee AFL-CIO introduced to me to T-Bone's, a place with the rare combination of a real functioning barbecue pit, country cooked vegetables, and a full bar. Talk about a place to go at the end of the day!

Of course, not every hotel is the Crowne Plaza and not every meal is at T-Bone's. I'll admit there are mornings when I wake up in some random hotel and it takes a few minutes to remember where I am. On the other hand, when I know friends or colleagues will be there, I feel lucky to be with people I admire and care about. Even more importantly, when I know my presence, my talk, my speech, or a workshop will help make a local event successful, I'm happy and proud to put up with life on the road. The exhilaration outweighs the exhaustion.

14

The 2004 Election

WHEN JOHN KERRY ran against George Bush for President in 2004, Andy Levin and I wanted to use that campaign to drive the need for the Employee Free Choice Act into the heart of the Democratic Party. We wanted to make workers' freedom to organize and bargain collectively a defining issue for Democrats just like healthcare, women's rights, and anti-discrimination. Andy came up with cards addressed to the Congress for workers and activists to sign. We began a huge drive to get them signed at every union event from January to November. On July 4th we connected political freedom to workplace freedom and then began to focus on the Democratic Convention in Boston.

We had a full-scale plan with absolute buy-in from the AFL-CIO staff. The day before the convention started, we held a huge teach-in and rally about the EFCA.

Massachusetts State AFL-CIO President Robert Haynes and his staff organized the leafleting of a reception sponsored by Verizon Wireless. We joined an event criticizing Verizon Wireless for their union busting. We wrote the Employee Free Choice Act into President John Sweeney's speech and sent two victimized workers onto the stage of the convention with him.

I was lucky enough to be on the floor of the convention when the tall, skinny State Senator from Illinois with the funny name who was running for the U.S. Senate took the stage. Barack Obama's speech was electric and thrilling. "We are not red states and blue states. We are the United States of America," he said, leaning into the microphone, raising the volume but not the pitch of his smoky voice. "Only in America," and he told his remarkable story. I turned to a woman standing next to me and said, "We're watching a political superstar being born." She agreed.

At the end of the week I wrote everyone in the AFL-CIO Organizing Department a partial victory memo: "Never has the Employee Free Choice Act been so prominently discussed and endorsed. This has been an historic week for us and our historic fight and campaign to win workers' freedom to form unions and bargain collectively." We had 100,000 cards signed for passage of the Employee Free Choice Act and were ready to drive straight and hard into the election campaign.

No Democrat can be elected President without carrying Wisconsin. Al Gore won Wisconsin in 2000, but only by 5,000 votes. I went there and began working with my good friend Bruce Colburn from the AFL-CIO. Greg Junemann, National President of the International Federation of Professional and Technical Employees, IFPTE, also joined me. Greg, who lived in Milwaukee, is both smart and principled and a boon to the American labor movement. Bruce and Greg seemed indefatigable. We spoke all over the state, connecting the Employee Free Choice Act and the health and vitality of the labor movement to the campaign, emphasizing the necessity to elect the Kerry-Edwards ticket. We phone-banked, leafleted worksites, and door-knocked union members. We traveled the state to every AFL-CIO and local union meeting we could squeeze into our schedules.

Two or three days before the election, Bruce and I stood on a bridge in downtown Milwaukee with twenty or thirty construction union activists and leaders. We were there to keep Bush rally attendees from disrupting a Kerry rally that included Bruce Springsteen. What seemed like the coldest rain I'd ever felt slammed us. We were soaked to the skin, shivering near hypothermia. A small crowd of Bushites tried to get past us, there was a tussle, and one of our guys had to be hustled away. That night I filled my truck with the 100,000 cards for the

Employee Free Choice Act and headed for Ohio to speak at the last rally of the campaign. For reasons I still cannot fathom, the country chose to endure four more years of George W. Bush. Wisconsin, however, went Democratic by 11,000 votes.

Through it all, we maintained our focus on encouraging and helping national unions train organizers, building the ranks of their organizers, and putting more resources into organizing. We at the AFL-CIO worked extensively with the Teamsters, Electrical Workers, Utility Workers, Ironworkers, UAW, American Federation of Teachers, Amalgamated Transit Union and several others. Our work paid off handsomely in 2007 and 2008 when the American labor movement grew by more, both in absolute numbers and in percentage of union members, than we had grown in a generation. Think about it: during George Bush's awful assault on unions and workers, we grew by more new members than we had in a generation. That is the power of organizing.

We had found the ingredients for growth, including investment by the AFL-CIO and national unions and pressure on employers to recognize their workers' rights to organize and bargain collectively. We worked at every level of government to create policy limiting employers' ability to retaliate against and terminate workers who wanted to form a union. We also knew we had to do real organizing work across national boundaries because so many employers are truly global. The labor movement has to be able to pressure employers in their home countries and to run multiple organizing campaigns against a single employer around the world. Only then can we realistically expect to stop the awful global economic race to the bottom and the corporatization of the world economy.

We have good global union federations, but they are, for the most part, not designed to assist in fighting employers in organizing campaigns. We need to make cross-border organizing regular and routine, rather than episodic. That is why we hosted the world's first-ever Global Organizing Summit in 2005. We invited organizing directors and colleagues from South Africa, Britain, Argentina, Germany, Japan, South Korea, and France for a global summit the day before our domestic organizing summit on International Human Rights Day. The meeting was incredibly productive. We had honest discussions about global employer intimidation of workers and the dangerous decline in union density all over the world. Ken Zinn and I talked at length about the Employee Free Choice Act and the necessity for workers in America and across the world to win the freedom to form unions and bargain collectively.

On the following day, we held our domestic organizing summit in Washington, D.C., with about 700 organizers and leaders from all over the American labor movement. As before, we focused the agenda on issues to be addressed for the American labor movement to grow. We needed adequate resources for organizing in order to have well trained and rigorously managed organizers. It was imperative to tie our politics to organizing. We also held a thousand-worker rally on Capitol Hill to call for passage of the Employee Free Choice Act.

Then, just as things were going so well, the wheels began to fall off the long-standing alliance among America's major labor unions. One of the most difficult periods in my life was beginning.

15

Exhausted and Heartbroken

THE HISTORICAL split in the AFL-CIO and the ill-fated founding of the meant-to-be rival federation, Change To Win, happened in 2005. We at the AFL-CIO believed political action was crucial to organizing. We worked hard to pass legislation making employer intimidation illegal and subject to significant penalties. Our political programs pushed for new rights to organize for home care workers, childcare workers, and public employees. In these and many other ways, we built a political system that respected the rights of employees to form a union and to bargain collectively. The leadership of Change to Win publicly rejected a role for politics in organizing, but I always have believed that was more of a smokescreen to justify the split, rather than a serious position and distinction. In any event, for whatever the reason, the decision by some of our largest affiliated unions to leave the AFL-CIO helped make 2005 one of the most unpleasant years in my life.

As the preliminaries to the split were upon us, we were still making progress on organizing and should have been pushing forward in a united and determined offensive. Instead, we were arguing over the arcane internal politics of the American labor movement. The 2005 March Executive Council meeting in Las Vegas was a nightmarish brew of personal spats and nasty, divisive debates. I couldn't believe it was happening. The American labor movement was splitting during the worst presidential and governmental assault against labor since Woodrow Wilson's notorious Attorney General Palmer raids in 1921 and 1922.

When it rains it pours. While all this was going on, my mother-in-law was diagnosed with pancreatic and liver cancer. My wife Mary Denham traveled to Savannah in March to help care for her. In the middle of all that, I had surgery on my left knee for a torn meniscus. I was very close to "Ms. Liz," as I called Liz Denham. Ms. Liz and I talked about my kids, Sam and Sydney, and the Bible and C.S. Lewis as we always did. Ms. Liz was a devout Christian and a determined progressive Democrat. She was a public and social Christian. Like me, she thought Jesus, the carpenter from Nazareth, was serious when He said, "Whatsoever you have done unto the least of these, you have also done unto me," or when He said, "Feed my sheep" or "Love your neighbor."

Within the space of four short weeks, I gave the eulogy at Ms. Liz's funeral and helped run the divisive AFL-CIO convention in Chicago. I hardly slept or relaxed that week in Chicago. I helped run the floor operation and handled all the media about the split. I sat on a raised platform at the side of the convention hall on Chicago's Navy Pier and monitored the floor. For media interviews and debates, a golf cart would whisk me to a relatively quiet media desk backstage.

Beyond all the institutional difficulties and complexities, things were made much worse because the Service Employees International Union, SEIU, one of the unions leaving the AFL-CIO, was my union. And many of the organizers and leaders of the other splitting unions were close friends. In 1982, I was the first organizer John Sweeney had hired at SEIU. I was on national staff when Andy Stern, SEIU's highly visible president, came on staff. I had helped build the organizing culture and program at SEIU. Bruce Raynor and Mark Fleischmann of UNITE HERE and I had been close friends for almost fifteen years in Atlanta. We had worked closely on campaign after campaign. By 2005 friends like Bruce Colburn and Mark Splain and Bill Ragen and Peter Ryder had left the AFL-CIO to work for SEIU.

I felt terrible the morning of the first day of the Chicago convention when I had to accept and sign for the letters of disaffiliation from SEIU and the Teamsters. That same night on PBS I had to debate a close friend, the Teamster's organizing director Jeff Farmer. Later in the week, the *Atlanta Journal-Constitution* ran a full-page story with pictures about my relationship with Bruce Raynor and the prominent roles we were playing on opposite sides of the split. On the second or third day of the convention, I was hustled off my raised platform to the media desk for a public radio debate with an SEIU operative about the split. Folks described me that week as constantly watching everything around me, unable to relax or let down. They didn't know the half of it.

The American labor movement split that week in the summer of 2005 in Chicago. Mercifully, the convention was finally over. The follow-up was another story. I was on the hot seat a lot, criticized by old friends and colleagues because our growth had stalled, and on a personal level for staying with the AFL-CIO. Institutionally, I was responsible for managing both the politics of the split and the media. I had to repeatedly debate folks whom I thought were wrong without criticizing their motives or the institutions they represented. I did about twenty public debates about the split, which were broadcast on NPR, Pacifica Radio Network, CNBC, and many other broadcast outlets, most of them with people I admired and respected from SEIU and the Teamsters. I also began handling every hostile media interview request that came into the AFL-CIO. That's how and when I started doing debates with TV hosts on Fox News and Fox Business.

I remember one day when CNBC called and asked me to debate Andy Stern that afternoon. I was wearing a Latin Guayabera shirt and told them I didn't have a tie. The producer asked if my shirt had a collar. I said yes, and she said, "You're fine." I thought again how unproductive and sad it was for us to debate when we could have been whaling on George Bush, the Republicans, and the Financial Elite. And, of course, employers smelled blood in the water and continued to challenge us at every turn. It was maddening and continuously heartbreaking to fight over organized workers instead of against bosses on behalf of unorganized workers.

And, still, the fight dragged on. My organizing department at the AFL-CIO had to help our affiliates beat back raids from the unions of Change to Win. SEIU tried to recruit AFSCME-organized home care workers in California. Dave Eckstein, on my staff, led a fight to defeat the Teamsters raid of Amalgamated Transit Union workers at the Chicago Transit Authority. By the end of 2005, we had successfully met almost all of the challenges to our membership. Our victories came at huge cost, however. That cost was measured in the workers we could have organized at such a critical time in labor's history.

The ridiculous internal fight in organized labor over issues the American public thought greedy and Byzantine, drove me crazy. It seemed like I was consumed with debates over the split and raids on our affiliates. We did our duty, soldiering up every day and winning fight after fight. But the battles we won were against other unions that I had come to respect so much during my years as a labor organizer. The year 2005, more than any other in my life, left me exhausted and heartbroken.

16

Turning up the Heat

WITH THE agony of the labor split finally behind me,
I was able to turn my full attention once again to what I
consider the most important labor legislation in a generation, the Employee Free Choice Act. The American public was finally turning against George Bush and the failed
policies he had used to bludgeon working families and
unions. We took full advantage. All across America, we
pressed our case for the Employee Free Choice Act and
the fundamental freedom of all workers in America to
decide for themselves whether to have a union and engage
in collective bargaining.

We began our campaign in 2006 by interviewing each
Congressional candidate concerning his or her stand on
the EFCA. When a candidate took a position against us,
we gave him or her a tutorial on the legislation. Of course,
we covered the issue and its importance to America's

working people, but we also told each candidate that backing the Employee Free Choice Act was essential if he or she expected any support from organized labor. One after another, Congressional incumbents and challengers, including some Republicans, signed on to support the Act. Believe me, there was quite the celebration at AFL-CIO headquarters on the day we reached 200 co-sponsors in the House of Representatives.

Finally, we were back to the real business of building and organizing the American labor movement and the AFL-CIO. With our help and encouragement, the United Mine Workers of America, the Amalgamated Transit Union, the Ironworkers, AFSCME, the Utility Workers Union, the International Brotherhood of Electrical Workers, the Painters, the Sheet Metal Workers, the American Federation of Teachers, the Communications Workers, the Steelworkers, and the United Auto Workers moved more resources into their organizing departments. Then, in October 2006, Karen Ackerman, the political director of the AFL-CIO, invited all the Democratic Congressional challengers to the AFL-CIO headquarters for a half-day briefing on our key issues. Pennsylvania's Joe Sestak and Patrick Murphy, Indiana's Brad Ellsworth, and thirty or so other key Democratic challengers listened intently as workers from several organizing campaigns told their horror stories of what happened when they tried to form a union and what lengths their employers went to stop them.

Meanwhile, I spent most of the election season in my native state of Tennessee working on the campaign to elect Congressman Harold Ford, Jr., who aspired to be the first African-American Senator from a southern state since Reconstruction. His father, Harold Ford, Sr., was a full-on political progressive when he was in the U.S. House. I worked alongside President Jerry Lee, Secretary-Treasurer Eddie Bryan, and lots of other wonderful folks with the Tennessee AFL-CIO. We were blessed with a fantastic candidate, too. I well remembered how great his father was as a candidate and Congressman when I was head organizer of Memphis ACORN almost thirty years earlier.

I was so proud of the labor movement in my native state. Stan Johnson, then the Southern Regional Director of the Steelworkers, and I had several conversations about how unlikely it would have seemed when we were growing up in Tennessee to see so many work so hard on behalf of an African-American candidate for the U.S. Senate. Scott Reynolds turned out crowds of 200 to go door-to-door in Nashville. Selwyn Carter had a crew of volunteers leafleting every shift change and door knocking every day in Memphis and Shelby County. Jimmy Hyde had a crew in Chattanooga that phoned, hit the doors, and leafleted every day. Clarence Frost oversaw it all. Jerry Lee, Eddie Bryan, and I were as many places as we could be, talking to as many workers as we could. We worked all day, ran to the next town for two or three or four hours, and started again every morning leafleting another shift change.

I criss-crossed the state, speaking at AFL-CIO events, at local unions, and while I passed out leaflets during shift changes. I talked about my youth, about my Tennessee family's values of a hard day's work for a decent day's wage, and about the Scriptures. During the times we appeared together, candidate Ford was such a Tennessee gentleman that I had to tell him not to call me "Mr. Acuff." My pride in watching my native state struggle so hard to elect an African-American Senator was matched only by my disgust at how our opponent, Bob Corker, played relentlessly on Tennessee's racist history. Political pitches reminiscent of the worst of Lee Atwater, Karl Rove, and Strom Thurmond carried the day for Corker by a small margin.

In spite of the Tennessee Senate race, 2006 was a great year for Democrats and the American labor movement. November brought us a pro-worker majority to the U.S. Congress and set up a legislative test for the Employee Free Choice Act. During the next few months, two of the great leaders of the modern labor movement began their strategy discussions. One was Larry Cohen, President of the Communications Workers of America and Chair of the AFL-CIO Organizing Committee. The other was President Leo Gerard of the Steelworkers and Chair of the AFL-CIO Legislative Committee. After many long and intense discussions, Larry and Leo decided to run the Employee Free Choice Act in the House of Representatives. In short order we were at Nancy Pelosi's celebration of her election as the Speaker of the House, circulating through the crowd as the Grateful Dead were playing, and asking members of the House of Representatives to wear stickers supporting the Employee Free Choice Act.

Union activists and leaders around America turned up the heat on Democratic members of Congress. Fred Azcarate, Eileen Toback, and I worked under intense pressure from Larry and Leo in an epic struggle to pass the Employee Free Choice Act. I intensified my already full travel schedule. Tim Waters and the Steelworkers made tens of thousands of phone calls to Congressional offices. Our efforts paid off in March of 2007 when the legislation passed Speaker Nancy Pelosi's House of Representatives 241-185. I cried, wept, and sobbed at the enormity of our victory.

17

Signs of Hope

SOMETIMES it is easy, too easy, to give up. By the mid-2000's, the unrelenting corporate and political assault on America's labor unions, along with our unprecedented internal strife, had taken their toll on morale. Many had given up on the chances of organized labor ever growing again. In times such as those, the organizer's most important job is to hold out hope. Time and again, I said the AFL-CIO Organizing Department had a plan that gave us a chance, not a guarantee, but a chance of growth. If we prosecuted that plan diligently, it would pay off. It did. In two years, we saw a net gain of 750,000 members. The American labor movement grew in both raw numbers and density by more than it had in a generation. Shocking as this was to observers of the American labor movement, I was not surprised.

How could this growth happen in such difficult times? Many things came together in ways that favored us. Unions continued to build their organizing efforts and focus on growth. State governors and legislatures enhanced the organizing rights for public employees and other workers not covered by the National Labor Relations Board. Our lead organizers redoubled their training programs that helped national unions win important organizing campaigns. We also benefited from growing support for the union, political, and social movement agitating for First Amendment Free Speech and Free Association Rights for workers. Our success with the Employee Free Choice Act was paying dividends that few of us expected.

The union growth of 2007 and 2008 was a tribute to human will and institutional perseverance and determination. Never underestimate the amazing willingness of average American workers to struggle collectively for justice, respect, and dignity. In 2008, my superiors at the AFL-CIO asked me to become Special Assistant to President John Sweeney for Organizing. The shift in job titles and responsibilities allowed me to focus more intensely and directly on the campaign to finish what I considered to be Job One, the passage of the Employee Free Choice Act. Fred Azcarate and I directed the campaign for Larry Cohen's brainchild, the mobilization of one million shop stewards in support of our legislative priority. By early 2009, over 1.5 million workers had signed cards calling on the new Congress and President to pass the EFCA.

Meanwhile, we had a new U.S. President to elect. The campaign to elect Barack Obama was unique in American history and in American labor history. Union activists and leaders across American stood up for racial justice and progressive politics. Bill Lucy, Secretary-Treasurer of AFSCME, said it all when he inspired the Machinist Union members with, "You can vote for a white enemy or a black friend." Across Pennsylvania with the Steelworkers, to Nurses' conventions, to Massachusetts and New Hampshire and Minnesota, to St. Louis and Cape Girardeau, from Missouri to Arkansas to Oregon to Kentucky and Tennessee, and everywhere else I could get anyone to listen, I reminded workers what was at stake in the 2008 election.

The Democratic National Convention was in Denver that year. Fred Azcarate, Jerry Acosta, and I were charged with speaking to every state caucus and every identity caucus in those few days. Our topic, of course, was the crucial importance of enacting the Employee Free Choice Act. That meant both early mornings and late nights. We reminded the delegates that the rights to form a union and bargain collectively were both an internationally accepted human right and an essential policy foundation for the strengthening of the middle class. I remember our presentation to the Illinois delegation particularly well. The Illinois delegation, always divided between Chicago and the rest of the state, had a new and even more divisive issue before them. Should the state add on to O'Hare Airport, which was under the control of Mayor Daley, or build a new airport in Congressman Jesse Jackson's district? With C-SPAN cameras rolling, Congressman Jackson made an emotional plea for Democratic Party unity. Then, with little notice or fanfare, Mayor Daley introduced me. I quickly took the podium and made my Employee Free Choice Act pitch as persuasively as I could in as short a time as possible. My friend Jerry Acosta, who was not in the room at the time, congratulated me the next day. When I asked how he knew what I had done, he told me how he woke up in the middle of the night, turned on C-SPAN, and there I was!

After the Convention we all went back to doing all we could to elect Barack Obama and a pro-worker Congress. I spent a lot of time in Georgia with another old friend, Jim Martin, who was running for the U.S. Senate. Our chances weren't good, but both Obama and Martin would be great friends of labor. I had known Jim since 1985 when I went to Georgia as a labor organizer. I was very fond of him. He had courageously supported our efforts to strengthen the union movement and every other righteous cause that came before the Georgia General Assembly. So clear was the righteousness of Jim's heart that I once told a small crowd in Washington, D.C., that Jim reminded me most of Atticus Finch in *To Kill a Mockingbird*. Obama lost Georgia, but Jim was in a run-off against radical rightwing incumbent Republican Saxby Chambliss. I quickly became the principal spokesperson for labor's campaign in Georgia. I was teamed with a brilliant, hard-working young political organizer named Courtney Pecquex who made sure I had plenty of media exposure. Despite our best efforts, Jim Martin lost his challenge to Saxby Chambliss.

However, the 2008 election brought us an even bigger majority in the House of Representatives. Support for the Employee Free Choice Act was stronger than ever. Now we turned our attention to the Senate, a much steeper hill to climb. We needed a super-majority there if we were to avoid rightwing minority filibusters. So, at the beginning of 2009, we set about getting the sixty votes we had to have to pass the Employee Free Choice Act in the U.S. Senate. We dispatched staff to Colorado, Montana, Indiana, Nebraska, Arkansas, Louisiana, Virginia, and Pennsylvania. I immediately hit the road to all those states, but most of the summer of 2009 found me in Arkansas and Louisiana. We held rallies and debates. We did TV and radio and visited newspaper editorial boards. I ran all over Arkansas trying to get Senator Blanche Lincoln right on the Employee Free Choice Act.

Then, on July 11, 2009, the Steelworkers' Tim Waters led 1500 of us in the biggest labor action in the history of Arkansas. Everyone cheered wildly in front of Central High School where Arkansas' schools had been first integrated when Steelworkers' president, Leo Gerard, and Arkansas African-American leader, Dr. Wendell Griffin, spoke. Then we marched two miles in the blazing, humid Arkansas sun to the State Capitol and another rally, finishing with a grand-scale catfish fry on the Capitol grounds.

My excitement at the Arkansas rally was soon over-shadowed by events that would open a new chapter in my life. John Sweeney retired as President of the AFL-CIO at the fall convention, and I did not expect to fare well in the changing of the guard. Nationwide, the struggling economy was setting the stage for the coming Republican landslide in the 2010 elections. More and more, it appeared that working Americans would have to wait longer for the Employee Free Choice and the rights to organize they deserved and so desperately needed.

18

Lessons Learned

TODAY, I serve as Chief of Staff of the Utility Workers
Union of America. I have the privilege of doing what I
have always done, and what I have always loved to do:
Organizing for a better America. I have told you much
about the road that brought me here, but not enough about
what I learned along the way. So I will end with some
thoughts for new organizers, the ones who will take up
the challenge of keeping power where it belongs, that is,
in the hands of ordinary working Americans.

First and foremost, don't forget what organizing
is about. It is about building power, pure and simple.
Too many of us are taught that power is somehow
unseemly or crass or impolite. It is not. In truth, power
is how you get things done, how you change things.
It's the whole purpose for organizing. Everything good
that has ever happened to or for average people is the

result of average people organizing and mobilizing together. Everything from America's independence to the destruction of slavery to the struggle of women for the right to vote to the end of legalized segregation to the creation of today's labor movement has happened because average, everyday people came together to fight for their rights.

As we work to build power, we must always remember the rich and powerful often create laws to keep themselves in place as society's elite. Because of this, effective organizers must always question authority. Who is exercising authority? In whose interest is the authority being exercised? What is the effect on average people? What is our appropriate response to the authority handed down from above? All human beings are due respect and dignity just because of their humanity, and not because of this or that law.

You will often find that accepting the need for power and questioning the authority held by powers-that-be is difficult. When you do, remind yourself of something that has inspired me time and again. You are not alone. Indeed, average people, everyday workers, will fight like hell for their own dignity. During a particularly difficult, intense, confrontational, and hostile organizing campaign, workers are motivated not by material issues, but by fundamental demands for dignity and respect.

American organizers are also continually challenged by the myth of the independent American hero. Remember that the most important events in American history were won not by in individuals, but by organizations of average people and the organizers who brought them together. Remember the privilege that awaits you of being one of those organizers. Faith in average people connected to the skill and discipline of a good organizer will make the change we all seek.

Let us now turn to some of the skills and attitudes that will help you along the way to becoming a good organizer. High on that list is this: Never substitute anything for personal communication. Organizing is all about communication, the deeper and more personal the better. Moving into collective action is foreign to most Americans. It must be constantly reinforced. The best place to do that is where the worker is most at home, the kitchen or den or porch. I spent a good part of my youth coon hunting in rural West Tennessee and still take pride in loving and understanding coonhounds. I know them all—Walkers, Plotts, Redbones, Black and Tans, Blueticks. That came in very handy as an icebreaker during the days I spent talking to corrections officers and other state workers in rural Georgia. I've even done house calls at a man's kennel talking about his dogs and in a barn talking to someone else about his horses. As Saul Alinsky said, "You start with where folks are."

When people hear the word "communication," they often hear "talking." The organizer must think of communication more as listening. Active listening is the foundation of organizing. It is the prerequisite of every other organizing skill. Active listening allows the organizer to find what will move her or his constituency and then identify who can lead the constituency. Active listening will help the organizer clarify the important issues in a campaign. This kind of listening is the key skill in the house call, home visit, or door knock. And, above all, you must be able to confidently and humbly sit with a worker in her or his home, listen, talk about issues, validate the pain and anger of the worker, and begin the process of moving workers to collective action.

Active listening will be your friend as you work to break down the many barriers between people. Gender, race, ethnicity, sexual orientation, age, neighborhood, religion, place of birth, and language can all be obstacles. Breaking down these barriers is essential if we are to restore balance and justice to the American economy and society. Bosses, dictators, despots, and every society's Financial Elite exploit the divisions between average people both to weaken them and to hang onto power and wealth. Your job as an organizer is to make sure their destructive, self-serving strategy of divide and conquer fails miserably.

Active listening will also help you validate the indignities and those blows to their self-respect your constituents suffer every day at work and in the broader world. Too many workers in America don't believe they are entitled as human beings to dignity and respect. Giving folks their God-ordained dignity and respect is incredibly powerful. The boss never does it. The good organizer always does it. My deceased friend Rev. James Orange, one of those closest to Dr. King, was so great at this. He called everyone "Leader" and appealed to the better angels in everyone. That is why Bill Lucy and the striking Memphis sanitation workers in 1968 carried signs that simply said, "I am a Man."

Work your ass off. Organizing requires great effort and long hours. You must be present. At the same time, resist doing anything for people that they can do for themselves. You cannot build a union or a community organization for others. They have to do it themselves, albeit with the organizer's facilitation and guidance and sometimes urging and pushing. Grassroots leaders must be found and identified and trained. Organizers have to give tasks to an organizing committee. If built only by outsiders, local unions and community organizations will melt like cardboard in a rainstorm in the face of certain conflict. A great woman organizer named Mo Fitzsimons used to say to workers,

"It is what it is and it won't change till you decide to change it."

You must be present when workers are available to talk. That means your day cannot end at five p.m. Organizing requires great will. The families of serious organizers pay a real price. I've learned that over and over the hard way. Organizers don't punch time clocks or fill out time sheets. When I was organizing for ACORN we knocked on doors every evening from four to eight p.m.—the time of the day when average folks are most reliably at home. Some of us attended church with our members, took meals with our members, and generally spent all kinds of time with our member and leaders and those we were organizing. When we were building the Georgia State Employees Union, SEIU Local 1985, our routine was to house call second shift workers from eleven a.m. till two p.m., then house call first and third shift workers from four to eight p.m., and finish the day with phone calls from eight to nine p.m. to remind folks about the next meeting.

Because the organizer's job is so demanding, you must always try to find some balance. None of us is super-human. The best organizers find ways to build a personal life while they are organizing. I am the first to admit how hard this is and how often I've failed at it. But it is essential if an organizer is to last more than a couple of years in the work. Until my children, Sam and Syd, were born, fishing

was my great escape. Now there is nothing better than
Sam and Syd except my life partner, Mary Kaye. Some
great life partnerships have been created in the white-hot
crucible of organizing, but just as many have fallen victim
to the incessant demands of life on the streets.

Organizers have a responsibility to prevent anything
from getting in the way of communicating with workers.
Inattention to dress, clothes, appearance, or behavior can
prevent that communication connection between worker
and organizer. Dressing appropriately does not mean
investing in lots of clothes. It simply means making certain that your appearance isn't off-putting or distracting
from your message and communication. You don't wear
a necktie to house call in South Georgia where no one
wears a necktie. On the other hand, you make sure you
are clean and neat. Think about to whom you are talking
and how you can make them most comfortable with your
presence and how your appearance will not distract from
the message. Overalls don't go over well in cities and sub-
urbs (and probably not any more in rural areas) and high
heel shoes and Armani suits don't go over well for house
calls anywhere.

Workers organize to win. Winning requires clear,
strategic thinking. It's the responsibility of the organizer to
either plan or guide a campaign's plan in a sharply strategic
manner. Most of us don't grow up thinking strategically. It

requires discipline, thinking without emotion, and forcing oneself to consider issues with as much clarity as possible. Any campaign, from union organizing to a contract fight to winning city services in a low income neighborhood, requires identifying and exploiting a target or an opponent's vulnerabilities. This identification and exploitation requires research. This is the key to giving an employer or a target enough incentive to do the right thing. Many things can constitute vulnerabilities. There may have been relationships with unsavory partners, a record of ignoble regulations or laws, or customer pressure, to name just a few of many possible examples.

Exploiting vulnerabilities almost always generates conflict. Conflict is inevitable in the clash of interests between workers and bosses or in cases of low-income residents and city governments. Do not shy away from conflict; rather, welcome it as a pre-condition for winning. It's the responsibility of the organizer to prepare and train those who've been organized for the conflict that's required for victory. Most of us are taught all of our lives to act politely so everyone will like us. How often have you heard, "You catch more bees with honey"? That may be true in our personal relationships, but not usually in campaigns to win. Almost always, success as an organizer involves conflict.

Of course, conflict can generate emotions. Anger, joy, depression, fear, embarrassment, and anxiety are natural.

If the organizer ever loses her or his righteous anger and indignation at injustice, it's time to find another vocation. Having those emotions and showing those emotions are two different things, however. The best way to kill an organizing campaign is for the organizer to show fear or too much out-of-control anger or depression or anxiety. The organizer must learn and understand how to modulate her or his emotions because the organizer lives in a fish bowl. The employer or target is watching you. Everyone you're organizing is watching you. You simply can't afford to expose yourself in a non-strategic manner. At the same time, there is another emotion you should always show. That is hope. Organizing is futile without the hope and belief that a unified people acting in concert can win. You gotta believe.

Every successful organizer will sooner or later have the opportunity to transfer the power built by the whole into personal power. This is always tempting and can be useful. Sometimes it's useful and good for the organizer to assume leadership. But for the most part, the organizer's role is to help workers create organizations, not to run organizations. The best way for us organizers to pursue our dreams and passions is for us to keep building organizations while training those who provide leadership to the campaign. The best way for us organizers to exercise leadership is with other, younger organizers who need training, support, and a sounding board.

I've saved the most important lesson of all until the end. It is not about concepts and techniques, as important as those things are. Only an enduring remembrance of why you are working so hard will get you through the toughest days and darkest nights as you teach people how to work together.

We organize to give people a voice. We organize people no one has listened to and give them a voice everyone has to hear. We organize for a place at the table of decisions. We organize to make the city council or the CEO take notice.

We organize for the common good. We organize for those things that make all of our lives better. We talk about the stop sign to slow down speeders and make the streets without sidewalks safer for our kids. We talk about how to make the job less difficult or dreary or dangerous.

We organize for power. We know that the only source of power for us is collective power, the power of our numbers. We organize because we've learned that power goes either to the Financial Elite or to average folks who've joined forces with one another.

We organize for justice for all Americans. I, and now you, can take our place in the lineage of those who worked with Tom Paine in Philadelphia and Sam Adams in Boston during our struggle for national independence, with Frederick Douglass and Sojourner Truth in their fight to rid the country of slavery, with Susan B. Anthony and Elizabeth Cady Stanton to win the right to vote for women, and with A. Philip Randolph, Dr. King, Rev. James Orange, Dr. Joseph Lowery, and Rev. Jesse Jackson to rid the country of racial segregation.

Well, that's it. I've told you how I did it. Now it's your turn. Hasta la Victoria!

I have come to
Connect myself
Ground myself
Root myself
In the unchanging
Immovable
Essential
And so I watch Ross Peak
That mountain
To better understand
How to stand
When the sun moves and
The light changes
When the clouds close or
Part
When the rain carries hail
And threatens
When the wind is angry
How to stand
Rooted to the eternal
Grounded in the essential

—*from* Changing Course